NORWEGIAN MUSIC A SURVEY

BY

KRISTIAN LANGE

TANUM-NORLI

OSLO

Second revised edition
© Kristian Lange 1982
ISBN 82-518-1654-8
Nikolai Olsens trykkeri a.s, Kolbotn

PREFACE

This book is basically a third and extensively revised edition of *Norwegian Music, A Survey*, which was published in 1958 by Dobson Books Ltd. of London. The second edition was published by Johan Grundt Tanum of Oslo in 1971. In this edition I have used the introductory chapters without making any changes, but the remaining chapters have been rewritten as far as was necessary. Chapter Five, *The Present Time*, is based on answers given by the composers themselves to questions I put to them regarding their education, the trends they consider themselves to be following, and those of their works they consider to be of particular significance. Also the sixth and last chapter, *Music in Norway Today*, had to be brought up to date.

I would like to thank all the persons and institutions involved for their valuable help, and particularly I feel extremely obliged to Jostein Simble and his staff at Norsk Musikkinformasjon, the Norwegian Music Information Centre.

Oslo, in February 1982

Kristian Lange

CONTENTS

Preface 5

Introduction 7

Chapter one
Folk-music.. 9

Chapter two
Grieg's forerunners 17
Notes to chapter two 28

Chapter three
Grieg and his contemporaries 29
Notes to chapter three 39

Chapter four
The inheritors 40
Notes to chapter four 51

Chapter five
The present time 53

Chapter six
Music in Norway today 134

INTRODUCTION

One need not travel far beyond the boundaries of Norway to realize that, for most people, Norwegian music is practically synonymous with the name of Edvard Grieg, and the farther one goes out into the world, the more marked is this association.

Since Grieg died in 1907, there have been more than fifty years of progress, years which in most countries have produced a remarkably rich and varied development in the world of music.

During these years Norway, too, has enjoyed her share of this advance, and fostered a succession of young and talented musicians who have carried on the heritage of Grieg and found inspiration in his works. Grieg, on the other hand, can hardly be said to have sprung from nowhere, or to be himself the mainspring of a movement. On the strength of his great gifts his name will for many years to come shine with undimmed and almost romantic glory, and Grieg the Composer will for all time remain a central figure in Norwegian music. But in this little book we hope to give an account of the developments which led up to Grieg and of contemporary trends.

Classical music in Norway is a comparatively recent growth, compared with most other European countries. It came to the surface during the Romantic Age, and flourished in an atmosphere of national sentiment, which owed its historical background to the movement for National Independence which gathered ever-increasing impetus in the nineteenth century and won its final victory in 1905. Those who marched in the van of this movement were men like Grieg, side by side with poets such as Björnson and Ibsen, and artists like Dahl, Tidemand and Gude.

To make up for the comparative youthfulness of our classical music, we have folk-music of great age and variety, peculiar to our country, and based on longstanding traditions.

This is essentially due to geographical reasons and doubtless also to Norway's history before national awareness was roused. The sharply divided valleys, the isolated hamlets where communities lived their own lives steeped in inherited customs, and hardly, if at all, affected by outside influences, were all contributory factors. But it is equally safe to say that such influences as did come from outside, in the persons of alien officials, who were often out of touch with the life of the people they administered, were so essentially different from local customs that no real assimilation was possible. There were of course some who, in a spirit of snobbishness, adopted something of what these outsiders introduced, but without any attempt to add native colouring to what they borrowed, as their aim was sedulous imitation of the ways of the 'genteel' classes.

Thus the earliest investigators, who, imbued with the fervour of national romanticism, set about collecting folk-music round about 1840, found an astonishingly rich fund of material, with markedly national features.

It was not only the investigators who were enthusiastic. The leading composers of the day eagerly adopted the material and allowed it to colour their compositions. It was precisely in this way that they became forerunners, preparing the soil in which Grieg's genius could flower: to appreciate this, one must understand the peculiarities of Norwegian folk-music, and trace its development in Norwegian classical music.

CHAPTER ONE

FOLK-MUSIC

How old is Norwegian folk-music?

It is not possible to give any exact answer to this question, nor can one say which is the older, the ballads or the instrumental music.

There is a great deal of evidence to suggest that many kinds of instruments were part and parcel of the daily life of the people far back in history. In Voluspå, from *The Older Edda* (which was probably written about A.D. 1000) the *Gjallar horn* is mentioned, and elsewhere Heimdal, who blew on the *Lur* (a long birchbark horn, not unlike the Alpenhorn). And again we can read of the merry Eggther who sat on a mound and played his harp. In the Yngling Saga we are told that King Hugleik had in his retinue all kinds of musicians, who performed on the harp, the *Gige,* and *Fele* (types of fiddle).

One of our leading experts on folk-music, Dr. Erik Eggen, has said: 'Not a few of our tunes for the *Hardingfele* (Hardanger fiddle—the youngest of our national instruments) can be shown to originate far back in the Middle Ages, in some cases through the immediate impression they give or through their archaic form, in others on account of their names and the legends associated with them.' In this pronouncement Dr. Eggen does not exclude the possibility that there are sung melodies which live on among the traditional tunes of the Hardanger fiddle.

We can form the best idea of the appearance of these old instruments from the various illustrations in our possession, chiefly from the wealth of wood carving that has come down to us. Amang the instruments which have been found is the *bronz lur,* which is probably the oldest: this type has been found in the course of archaeological excavations both in Norway, at Jæren, and in Denmark, and has also been depicted in rock

The Langeleik   Photo: Norsk Telegrambyrå

carvings dating back to about 1000 B.C. The lurs that have been found are of bronze, and are estimated to date from the second century B.C. Besides these, it must be assumed that others of the known Norwegian instruments, like the *Bukke-horn* and *Neverlur, Munnharpe* and *Selje-flöyte,* were in use in the distant past.

The oldest preserved fragment of a harp is from the fourteenth century. The instrument is often in evidence in carvings found in our Stave Churches.

The name '*harp*' was used for several types of stringed instruments of different shapes, and with varying numbers of strings. It was also used to describe the *Langeleik,* which in Valdres was called the 'long harp'. This is shown, for instance, in a description of this instrument given by L. M. Lindeman in 1848:

"The langeleik, which has seven and sometimes more strings, is tuned by screws, *hörpöstillera,* which are set in the neck, in-

10

serted at each end. The short strings are tuned by these screws and also by means of the adjustable bridges. Along the outer string is a finger-board with small attached strips of bone or *hörpönota*, which form the scale. The instrument is played with a plectrum, or as we read: 'The *fjöröpin* is used for plucking the strings on the long harp or langeleik'."

The youngest of the essentially Norwegian instruments is the Hardanger fiddle. It is believed to have developed into its present form between 1550 and 1650—the oldest specimen preserved is to be found in the Museum at Bergen and is dated 1651. In some parts of the country it is called the *gigja* and it is possible that the instrument is a cross between the old Norwegian *gigja* and *fidla*.

The special feature of the Hardanger fiddle is that apart from the four strings found on an ordinary violin there is another set of strings set below, which vibrate in sympathy. The origin of these sympathetic strings can be described as traditional but it might also have been borrowed from abroad, where there were several types of instrument with similar undertones, such as the Scottish bagpipes, the Drehleier from Central Europe, and the Viola d'Amore.

These sympathetic strings on the Hardanger fiddle have made the shape of the instrument somewhat different from that of an ordinary violin. The neck is broader and a little shorter, while the peg box is longer in order to make room for the four extra pegs. The back is more arched and the belly higher.

The fiddle is usually much more ornate than an ordinary violin, both neck and soundbox being richly decorated with inlaid silver and mother-of-pearl, and the end of the tail-piece is often elegantly carved.

Finally, the bridge is higher than that on a violin, to allow for the underlying strings, but it also has a less pronounced curve on top, to enable the player to use the bow on as many as three strings at once.

On the old Hardanger fiddle the number of strings varied: both three and four upper strings are found and the number of understrings varied from two or three up to six. But the final version has four of each. In the *slåtter* (dance melodies) the

11

The Hardanger fiddle   Photo: Norsk Telegrambyrå

tuning of both upper and lower strings varies: there are various *stille* (ways of tuning), as the fiddlers put it.

In the tuning of the upper strings we find a long series of variations, e.g.

Folk dancing to the Hardanger fiddle at Norsk Folkemuseum, Bygdøy
Photo: P. A. Røstad-Foto

The understrings are usually tuned to the Do Re Mi Sol belonging to the major chord. Edvard Grieg's 'Morning', from the *Peer Gynt* suite, it will be seen, opens with these four notes.

There is no reason to doubt that song has just as ancient traditions among the Norwegian people as instrumental music, and there is a great deal of evidence to show that this is so.

Songs are frequently mentioned in the Sagas, and even if there is no proof of this, it is highly likely that the lays of the ancient scalds were sung, "for there is no known instance, in olden times, of a separate existence of poetry and melody" (Dr. Olav Gurvin). In Iceland they have tunes allied to *Eddakvad* and the verses of the scalds, and the Faroe Islanders have the 'song-dance', which dates back to the early Middle Ages.

In Norway too these have parallels, and we know that our oldest folk-songs, such as that great epic, the visionary *Draumkvæde,* go right back to the twelfth century. Many of our *kjempeviser* (giant songs) and other folk-songs possess the characteristics cited by Dr. Eggen, which naturally leads us to suppose that they have been known to the Norwegian people from medieval times.

When, about a hundred years ago, the task of writing down our folk-music was first tackled, the editors were from the outset faced with difficulties. They were trained musicians, accustomed to the normal harmonies and the usual major and minor keys. But in folk-music they found a different kind of tonality and intervals. In the development of musical expression in folk-music, natural intervals have played an important part—on these were based the notes of the lur and the other wind instru-

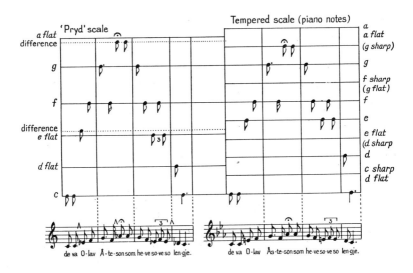

14

ments mentioned above. While major and minor keys have tones and semitones, the lur also includes three-quarter intervals, used where in ordinary music we would find semitones. Many of our airs for the Hardanger fiddle are written for this scale, and this has often been described as the Lydian mode.

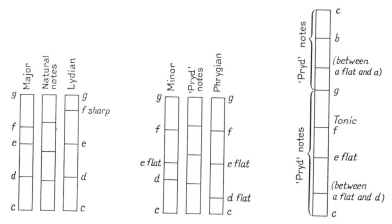

A contemporary Norwegian composer who has succeeded in capturing the true spirit of our folk-music, Eivind Groven, has written an account of this interpretation and arrived at a pattern for it (see illustration).

He shows an analogy in the minor keys, where the three-quarter interval gives a scale similar to the so-called Pryd system (decorative). This scale was interpreted as Phrygian, but Groven's schema (q.v.) shows the true relationship.

In a letter to a colleague who had written down some of the old airs, Grieg says: "It is remarkable, as you say, this G sharp in D major, it's something for the investigator". The augmented quarter-tone can also be heard in the peasant's song, "a ghost from some old scale or other".

Nowadays, on the Hardanger fiddle and the ordinary fiddle, old traditional dances are for the most part played: the *Springar* in three-four time, the livelier *Halling* in even time; the *Gangar*, a stately six-eight measure; and the bridal marches, still heard as in the past when the fiddler leads the bridal procession to and from the church.

Besides these recognized dances, we also have examples of the so-called *Lyarslåttar,* composed as 'pure' music and not intended as a dance accompaniment. Many of the folk-songs were —and still are—accompanied by a dance, especially those with a frequently repeated chorus, in which all the dancers join while a song leader sings the verses.

The lur, bukkehorn and related instruments have been much used for signals and for calling home the cattle: it is in fact highly likely that this was their original use.

Calling home the cattle has also provided the basis for many melodies, and even developed special forms of song such as *hauking* and *liljing.* And besides these we find, among the thousands of folk-songs that have been written down, all kinds, legends of the Middle Ages and the troll songs, songs of knights and giants from the sagas, songs of birds and beasts, comical ditties, lullabies and religous folk-tunes; and later songs whose writers can be identified, but which are just as alive on the lips of the people—and in their hearts.

CHAPTER TWO

GRIEG'S FORERUNNERS

As mentioned in the previous chapters, it was about a hundred years ago that the first serious attempts were made to write down Norwegian folk-music. This not only coincided with general trends in European art and literature; it was also due to special circumstances in Norway at the time. The nineteenth century was a restless time everywhere, with many intellectual cross-currents and shifting influences in art. The main impact was that of the Romantic age with its predilection for the remote and the obscure, its interest in nature, its search for origins, its taste for the middle ages, for adventure and the out-of-the-ordinary. All this had a strong influence on Norwegian intellectual life, and soon we find Norwegian works similar to those of the brothers Grimm and Herder.

But as far as Norway is concerned, the years between 1814 and 1905 were essentially a period of fermentation, a time of striving towards national self-expression, both intellectually and politically.

It bred, naturally enough, a keen interest in national characteristics of all kinds, a steadily increasing flow of enthusiasm for everything peculiarly Norwegian, not least for native arts and crafts.

The preceding generation had already 'discovered' the Norwegian peasant and his characteristic music; some composers—including foreigners who had settled in the country—had used folks-songs as themes for variations. In the musical play, *Fjeld-eventyret* (Mountain Adventure), with music by Waldemar Thrane and text by Bjerregaard, where the action takes place in the countryside, the composer employs the Norwegian folk-tune style to provide local colour in a musical setting which in every other respect is typical of contemporary Central Europe.

2

Statue of Ole Bull, Bergen

Photo: Mittet

But as mentioned in the introductory chapter, it was in those years that music as a conscious form of art was born in Norway, and it is most significant that the first in time of the three personalities who dominate Norwegian music before Grieg was an ardent nationalist, not only in his music but perhaps even more forcefully in other forms of national self-expression.

Few figures in the history of our music glow with the romantic brilliance of *Ole Bull*. This dazzling artist is numbered with the great virtuosi, with Liszt and Paganini, with whom he was often compared in his sensational international career as a violinist. His whole appearance and bearing compelled attention. "A finer figure of a man than Ole Bull could hardly have existed in his day", writes Jonas Lie. "Slender, well-proportioned strong and tall, he could be regarded as the ideal pattern for his countrymen. Thanks to a frugal and moderate way of living he retained a healthy slimness to the end of his days, with a waist like a young man's; yet he had a giant's chest and arms with muscles steeled by tireless plying of his bow. His expressive eyes shone with a strange mixture of simple childish trust and of the quizzical suspicion that is often a sign of genius."

He must have fascinated those who met him too with his keen intelligence, his many plans and wide interests. With the dazzling success of his romantic career thrown into the scales, he helped his countrymen in various ways to gain a measure of self-confidence. He was one of those that most clearly realized and asserted the intrinsic value of the arts peculiar to Norway. But he knew too how difficult was the task of translating idealistic plans into practical projects.

He was influenced by his vision of national self-expression from his youth onwards. In his excellent little book, *Ole Bull og norsk folkemusikk* (Ole Bull and Norwegian Folk-music), Arne Björndal describes how Ole Bull, from his boyhood days, was deeply enthralled by the fiddlers he met both in Bergen and out at the family's country place at Valestrand. Later, when re-visiting Norway, he was always keen to meet fiddlers and he would get them to play their *slåtter* for him. Usually he would sit apart and make notes.

He was above all a keen admirer of Myllarguten (the Miller's Boy, a famous country fiddler). He played in concerts with him, and supported him in a great many ways; and when, in 1850, Ole Bull was able to open his Norwegian Theatre in Bergen, Myllarguten was naturally one of those who joined him.

This theatre was Ole Bull's greatest achievement in the service of Norwegian art, his favourite dream that he had cherished during his years abroad, and which he proceeded to realize as soon as he returned from his sensational tour of America in 1848.

It was to be a genuinely Norwegian theatre—with Norwegian actors, Norwegian composers, Norway's poetry and Norway's own music. "The second of January 1850 will always be remembered as the Birthday of the Norwegian Stage and as Ole Bull's Day", says Jonas Lie in his monograph on Ole Bull.

In 1861 Henrik Ibsen was engaged by the theatre, first with a view to "assisting the theatre as a playwright" and later as producer. During the five years he worked there, Ibsen wote four plays for the theatre, among them *Fru Inger til Östråt*.

Björnstjerne Björnson worked there from 1857 to 1859 as *chef de théâtre,* and it was here that many of our outstanding national artists began their careers.

As a composer we can hardly say that Ole Bull ranks high in the history of Norwegian music. Not many of his pieces which he used to play at his concerts have survived him. But it is characteristic that his best-known melody, one which will undoubtedly endure as a true Norwegian folk-tune, *Sæterjentens Söndag* (Sunday on the mountain farm) expresses exactly his inmost Norwegian self, and the never-failing love and longing for his native land, in which lay the deepest roots of his art, and which proved a constant source of strength and renewal.

When King Frederick VI of Denmark asked him from whom he had learned to play, his answer was typical: "I learned from the mountains of Norway". For his unshakeable faith in our national values, Ole Bull will always mean much to us. "Ole Bull provided the first and greatest solemn occasion in the life of our people. He gave us self-confidence, the greatest gift he could have given us at that time", said Björnson in his speech at Ole Bull's funeral.

Ole Bull was a true torchbearer. But his hectic, restless life gave him neither the time to absorb the vast material which native music presented, nor the leisure to apply himself to the great task of adaptation which alone could have provided a source of fruitful inspiration to Norwegian classical music. It was in this respect that a contemporary, his junior by two years, *Ludvig Mathias Lindeman,* so excellently supplemented the work of the great virtuoso.

As personalities they were poles apart. Lindeman had not "learned from the mountains of Norway", but from the great masters of Central Europe, principally J. S. Bach. The Lindeman family, a remarkable parallel to the Bach family, were steeped in the traditions of European music with a strong interest in church music.

But even if L. Lindeman had not "learned from the mountains of Norway" these were to prove a significant factor in his life. Though he was an outstanding authority on church music, his most significant contribution, in a larger context, was the work that laid the real foundation of a study of Norwegian folk-music.

During the most impressionable years of his youth, he had made the acquaintance of Asbjörnsen and Moe's collection of Norwegian folk-tales, which inspired him with the same longing to unearth all the national treasures which he sensed lay concealed in Norwegian folk-music. And when he set to work, it was soon apparent that, with his forthright and pious nature, and his complete disregard for his own creature comforts, he was unusually well qualified for the task.

In his travels all over the country he collected over 1,000 folk-tunes. The first collection he published was *Norske Fjeldmelodier* (Norwegian Mountain Melodies adapted to Harmony), 1840. From 1848 onwards the results of his patient editing began to appear in the monumental key work, *Aeldre og nyere Norske Fjeldmelodier* (Norwegian Mountain Melodies Old and New). This contains about 600 tunes. The rest of his collection which has not been published, can be found in the collection of Norwegian Music in the University Library in Oslo, where it may be studied by music-lovers.

He has arranged most of the melodies as simple four-part songs; and many critics have found fault with the simplicity of his arrangements, which are frequently somewhat stereotyped. But in comparing them, as we tend to do, with Grieg's brilliant compositions, so national in their various movements, we must remember that Lindeman lived a generation before Grieg, and was besides strongly influenced in his musical education by Central European traditions. He has given some of the melodies a more elaborate arrangement, notably the thirty *Kjempeviser* (giant songs) for mixed choir, where he has given free rein to his great skill in counterpoint. And the arrangement of 'Draumkvædet' stands out as one of the greatest pieces of craftsmanship we have in Norwegian music.

Lindeman also wrote music for the ballads collected by Landstad and Jörgen Moe, and published a book of tunes for Seip's Songbook, setting his own melodies to a series of songs. Some of these, such as 'Millom bakkar og berg' and 'No livnar det i lundar' are so true to type that they can fairly be classed as folk-songs.

The other field where Lindeman made his mark on his own and following generations is that of sacred music. He was a first-class organist. When, in 1871, he visited London by invitation, together with other European organ virtuosi, to assist at the inauguration of the huge new organ in the Royal Albert Hall, his exquisite improvisations caused a sensation. He has also composed a number of organ works both larger and shorter ones.

But his greatest contribution to sacred music was undoubtedly the publication in 1877 of a book of hymn-tunes for Landstad's hymnal; this was officially adopted for use in the Norwegian Church. It contained 61 hymns for which he had composed his own tunes. Altogether he composed several hundred hymn tunes, of which some of the most beautiful and best-loved are 'The Church is an ancient dwelling', 'When mine eyes, weary of woe' and 'Easter's dawning ends our mourning'.

Halfdan Kjerulf   ·   Photo: Norsk Telegrambyrå

L. M. Lindeman, with his son Peter, also founded the Conservatoire of Music in Oslo.

Lindeman's collections of folk-tunes taught both his contemporaries and later generations to appreciate the wealth of music which still lived on among the people and which had come down to them from the early Middle Ages: and this was not the least important stimulus to national pride. Norwegians were no parvenus. In their folk-tunes at any rate, they possessed traditions as old as those of most countries in the world. These collections of folk-melodies were first and foremost an invaluable source of inspiration to the outstanding composers who joined hands with Lindeman in shaping a truly Norwegian type of music, men such as Halfdan Kjerulf and Rikard Nordraak.

Of the 1815 generation *Halfdan Kjerulf* is probably the composer whose music is most vigorously alive today, and whose name is still most truly a household word. He represents typically Norwegian music just as truly as any of the other composers. This is in a way remarkable, for neither by birth, upbringing nor inclination could Kjerulf be notably 'Norway-minded'. With Ole Bull nationalism was a principle; with Lindeman it was an object of research; with Kjerulf it was mainly the hue that art instinctively borrowed from the age, even where no set programme was professed. Kjerulf belonged to an old Danish family of civil servants, members of the so-called intelligentsia. He was a typical exponent of urban culture, living most of the time in the capital and even in his holidays travelling little about the country. For this reason he had no intimate, direct contact with folk-music—most of what he learnt he owed to Lindeman's collections. Yet there is a strongly marked Norwegian quality in most of his music—not only in the songs, where the words themselves may suggest a national mood.

In the fairly comprehensive correspondence he left behind, we can follow his development from an attitude of comparative indifference to national impulses during the time when he was influenced by the interests of his milieu, to a steadily growing active desire to create a specifically Norwegian art.

24

Rikard Nordraak   Photo: Ragnar Utne

He was at first at loggerheads with the militant nationalist group including Wergeland and Björnson, but in answer to criticism levelled at him by this circle he wrote, in 1859: "And now they're telling me there isn't a Norwegian note in my head . . . and yet they have the Songs of Arne [songs to words taken from Björnson's peasant tale *Arne*] ringing in their ears". And a little later, "So I told him that I was Norwegian in my own way and had at that very moment in the press a whole collection of Norwegian songs, including five of Björnson's. So they can see, I said sarcastically, whether the man from Leipzig is still very much a Leipzig man".

The Norwegian note in his music emerges at a very early stage. One can point to no special feature, no pattern germane to folk-music, it is something that cannot be defined, but it is there, permeating his work.

Halfdan Kjerulf was essentially a writer of lyrics, and above all he knew how to interpret Nature's many moods. He confined himself always to the small format, not only in his songs, but also in his piano pieces, which are all of the type to which Grieg subsequently applied the term 'lyrical pieces'. The most numerous of his works, as well as the most notable, are the songs, which contain a host of fine descriptive pieces, full of poetry and music, both in their lovely airs and their colourful piano accompaniment. Not without reasons has he been called 'The Norwegian Schubert'.

In his lifetime Kjerulf's contribution was not least important in his pioneer work in the choral field, and his many fine songs for male voice choir still exercise a refining influence in this genre. The delicate delineation of each part and the fine tonal treatment make great demands on a choir. It is not surprising that many of his songs for male voice quartet are still frequently performed.

Among Grieg's forerunners mention must be made of another, by no means the least of them, *Rikard Nordraak,* who was born only a year before Grieg. His life was short and uneventful on the surface but unusually rich in spiritual conflict.

In the twenty-four years of his brief life, he evolved a firm conviction of his own vocation, and also of the task facing

Norwegian composers at the time. His greatest service to Norwegian music was that he infected his contemporary Grieg with his own unshakeable faith in the intrinsic value of native music.

When Nordraak died, alone in Berlin, in 1866, much of the work he had set himself was still unaccomplished, but by his association with Grieg he had formed in his own image the man who in such rich measure was to fulfil his great promise.

In a letter to his father Rikard Nordraak professes his musical faith as follows:

They talk of carrying rocks to Norway but we have enough rock. Let us use simply what we have. Nationalism, in music for example, does not mean composing more Hallings and Springars such as our forefathers composed. That is nonsense. No, it means building a house out of all these bits of rock and living in it.

Listen to the unclothed plaintive melodies that wander, like so many orphans, round the countryside all over Norway. Gather them about you in a circle round the hearth of love and let them tell you their stories. Remember them all, reflect and then play each one afterwards so that you solve all riddles and everyone thinks you like his story best. Then they will be happy and cleave to your heart. Then you will be a national artist.

When he was seventeen or eighteen years old, Nordraak met Ole Bull, and wrote in his diary: "In his presence one feels the nearness of God". It is easy to imagine how Ole Bull's ideas enthralled his susceptible nature: in the same way L. M. Lindeman's collections must have been a great joy to him.

Otherwise he had little direct contact with Norwegian folk-music. Grieg so aptly describes the Norwegian atmosphere in his songs as "The result of great originality and an inborn sympathy with the spirit of our folk-music—which, as he said himself, he never really got to know and never had the time to absorb".

As a composer Rikard Nordraak was not prolific, but there are gems among his songs, and he will for all time be remembered as the man who wrote the music to Norway's National Anthem.

Bull, Ole Bornemann (1810—1880). Born in Bergen. Had no recognized musical education, but played the violin for a time with J. H. Paulsen and M. Lundholm in his home town. Was also in contact with local fiddlers. Made his first public appearance when nine years old. 1830 to Paris, where he developed his virtuoso technique. Gave concerts in various European towns in years after 1835. America 1851. American citizenship 1853. Lived mostly in America, visiting Norway every summer. Founded the first Norwegian theatre, 'Den Nationale Scene', Bergen 1850. Compositions: mainly virtuoso violin works performed by himself, including *Polacca guerrièra,* a violin concerto, variations on a theme of Bellini, *Sæterbesöget.* 'Sæterjentens Söndag' from *Sæterbesöget,* and 'I ensomme stunder' for four-part male voice choir are still frequently performed.

Lindeman, Ludvig Mathias (1812—1887). Born Trondheim. Grounding in music from his father who was organist. At 11 deputized for his father at High Mass. Began to study theology, discontinued on becoming organist at Vår Frelsers Church in Oslo 1839. Caused sensation with his playing and improvisation at the inauguration of new organ in Royal Albert Hall, London. After 1848 travelled round Norway collecting folk-melodies. Compositions include 36 Preludes and Fugues, three fugues on Bach themes, variations on 'Hvo ene lader Herren råde', and many hymn tunes including 'Kirken den er et gammelt hus' and 'Påskemorgen slukker sorgen'. Folk-melody collections include: *Norske Fjeldmelodier* (1841), *Aeldre og nyere norsk Fjeldmelodier* (1853—67), *Halvhundrede Norske Fjeldmelodier* (male voice choir) (1862), *30 Norske Kjæmpevisemelodier* (3 parts) (1863).

Kjerulf, Halfdan (1815—1868) born Oslo. Taught first by Lars Roverud and Otto Wetterstrand. Received grounding in composition 1848 from Carl Arnold, German musician resident in Oslo. 1849 received scholarship. Studied with Gade in Copenhagen and Richter in Leipzig. Lived mostly in Oslo as music teacher and critic. With J. G. Conradi ran the Subscription Concerts (first Norwegian concerts with symphony orchestra) 1857—9. Compositions: about 100 romances; 30 songs for male voice choir, piano pieces, music for Wergeland's *Söcadetterne iland,* piano arrangements of folk-tunes.

Nordraak, Rikard (1842—1866) born Oslo. Cousin of Björnstjerne Björnson. First musical training from H. Neupert in Oslo. Later studied under G. L. Gerlach, Copenhagen, and T. Kullak and F. Kiel, Berlin. Died of tuberculosis at 23. Compositions: Music for Björnson's *Maria Stuart* and *Sigurd Slembe,* 'Olav Trygvason', 'Ja, vi elsker', for male voice choir, some romances and piano works. Complete works edited by Ö. Anker and O. Gurvin.

CHAPTER THREE

GRIEG AND HIS CONTEMPORARIES

As we said in the Introduction to this survey, one does not have to travel far beyond the frontiers of Norway to realize that, for most people, Norwegian music is practically synonymous with the name of Edvard Grieg. No matter how far you travel outside Grieg's own country, you will have a fair chance of hearing his music; and if you talk to people who are at all interested in music, they will most probably be able to name works by Grieg which they know well. There are even biographies of him in English and other major languages.

In accordance with the overall plan of this survey, we consider it sufficient to include Grieg in the general line of development, mentioning the characteristic traits of his music and showing how, in due course, they provided an ideal, or at least a natural point of departure for the composers who followed him.

What is only hinted at in Kjerulf's music (see Chapter 2) is the essential element in Grieg's, and it is this that gives it its distinctive character. Grieg was deeply in love with everything Norwegian, both the country itself and the various aspects of its folklore: costumes, wood carvings, songs, and the music of the national instruments.

It was Rikard Nordraak, the last of the composers mentioned in the previous chapter, who really convinced Grieg that there was a wealth of material to be derived from Norwegian folk music. He made Grieg aware of this in the course of the 1860's, when Grieg had just graduated from the Leipzig Conservatory. He was rather bewildered by all the rules of German musical theory, and although he had the greatest respect for them, they were quite alien to his own creative intention, and therefore at first of little use to him as a composer. Nordraak's enthusiasm for and unshakable faith in the spirit of Norway encouraged

Grieg enormously, and gave him confidence in himself, his talent and his chosen style.

Through the years to come he set to work to become more deeply acquainted with Norwegian folk music, and adapted its peculiar characteristics to his own use. Typical Norwegian dance rhythms became more and more pronounced in his compositions, and in his melodic form there are echoes of the idioms of folk melodies. A great deal of his music is inspired by that of our national instrument, the Hardingfele, and in this connection one of the greatest living authorities on Norwegian folk music, Dr. O. M. Sandvik, has the following to say:

"Grieg has an extremely close connection with the Norwegian folk tune. He, who never borrows, sings in a way which makes us feel even his strangest melodies as unmistakably Norwegian. There are few of the peculiar traits in our folk music which do not have parallels in Grieg's melodic pattern. We meet the unruly coloratures of the mountain calls, the enchantment of the humorous songs as well as the grandeur and the solemnity of the hymns and epic songs. He is just as familiar with the placid lines of the dance-tunes from eastern Norway as he is with the intricate polyphony of the music for the Hardingfele. When his melody harks back to archaic layers of folkloristic expression, he touches the basic soil of the Norwegian folk tune."

Without going too far into structural details or analyses we can elaborate somewhat on what Sandvik means about Grieg's melodies. His music is characterised by frequent shifting between major and minor, and this instability of mode is so striking that one often wonders whether certain passages are in fact in a major or a minor key. The thirds of the folk scales are often unstable, wavering between major and minor. The Norwegian folk scales also employ other variable intervals, such as major or minor sevenths or perfect or augmented fourths. The older modal scales are just as important for the structure of typical Norwegian tunes as are the usual European major and minor.

But it is his harmonies above all which tell us, when we are listening to his music, that "this must be by Grieg". Grieg himself once said: "The realm of harmony has always been my

Nina and Edvard Grieg

dream world, and the feeling of harmony a divine mystery to me."

Both musicologists and composers stress that it was especially in the field of harmony that Grieg took a longer and bolder stride into the future than was realised at first. In his book *Music in the Romantic Era* Alfred Einstein maintains:

"Many of Grieg's ideas, in their boldness and tenderness, began to step over the borderline of "impression", and a history of post-Wagnerian impressionism would have to concern itself with him as one of its ancestors, or at least one of its godfathers."

In an article published in Paris in 1946 the French musicologist R. Bernhard says that "there is no doubt that Debussy and Ravel took up his (i.e. Grieg's) discoveries. His piano concerto, for instance, anticipates to an astonishing extent Debussy's harmonic and pianistic style." Finally, it should be mentioned that in 1926 Ravel himself corroborated Bernhard's statement, saying that "I have never to this day written a work that was not influenced by Grieg."

To an outside observer, Grieg would perhaps appear to bear the torch alone, but in reality other composers from the same period must be associated with the master. One name above all others is coupled with his as naturally as one connects the poets Ibsen and Björnson, and that is Johan Svendsen.

Johan Svendsen and Edvard Grieg complement each other. What Grieg gives us in the more intimate format Svendsen provides on a symphonic level. Together they fulfil, completely and triumphantly, the promise of Nordraak. They create 'Norwegian classical music on the basis of folk-music'.

Even though Svendsen's compositions are not entirely based on the music peculiar to Norway, as are Grieg's, it is his great achievement that he demonstrated the scope our native music offered as material for symphonies. At least one symphony (1861—62) by Otto Winter-Hjelm (1837—1931) had been written before Svendsen's, but Svendsen is popularly regarded as Norway's first symphonic composer, and his two works in this genre are without doubt still the most played of Norwegian symphonies. Their themes are unmistakably in the Norwegian idiom, and his thematic development is subtle and expressive. This is still more marked in his four Norwegian Rhapsodies and in his other adaptations of folk-tunes—they are of the same calibre as Grieg's many adaptations of Norwegian folk-melodies.

A warm bond of friendship existed between the two composers, and Grieg, in 1871, eloquently expressed the debt he owed to Svendsen in these words: 'He has taught me to have confidence in myself and in the power and rights of the individual—there are few artists to whom I feel indebted as I do to Svendsen.'

That Johan Svendsen, of the two, was to be so pre-eminently the composer of orchestral music is due to the circumstances of his life from his boyhood. Through his father, a military bandsman in the capital, he soon became familiar with various orchestral instruments and played several of them besides the violin, which his father concentrated on teaching him. He began at an early age playing at dances. At the age of fifteen he joined a military band. Strong, hard-working and keen, he also played in the theatre orchestra. His biographer, Aimar Grönvold, tells how, when he was engaged to play at one of the town's dancing schools, he used for the fun of it to adapt the most complicated études of Kreutzer and Paganini to dance rhythms.

Svendsen learned theory from the German musician Carl Arnold, who had settled in Norway, and before he went abroad at the age of twenty, he had tried his hand as a conductor.

Johan Svendsen's First Symphony was written while he was still a student at the Leipzig Conservatory. Before completing it he had composed an octet, but had not plucked up courage enough to show it to his teacher, Professor Reinecke, for in it he had given rein to his personal, already well developed ideas, which differed in various ways from what the Professor taught. But his fellow students were so enthusiastic about the octet that at last he let Reinecke see it. Somewhat ruffled that his pupil had kept the work to himself the Professor commented with some sarcasm: 'I suppose you will bring me a symphony next time, Herr Svendsen?'

And that is just what Svendsen did. Reinecke frankly admitted that his pupil had now clearly left the Conservatory stage behind—after three and a half years' study in Leipzig, Svendsen left the Conservatory with the Medal of Honour.

The Octet quickly found its way into the concert halls of Germany and the Symphony was also well received. When it was performed for the first time in Norway, in the Christiania Musical Society, an anonymous reviewer, who turned out to be Edvard Grieg, wrote:

Volumes could be written on the Symphony. . . . The outstanding merit of this Symphony is the complete balance between theme and technique. Svendsen makes great demands on his audience, carrying them off with him into a fantastic fairyland of whimsy and romance. But he gives them no choice; whether they want to accompany him on his journey or not, his listeners are, as it were, forcibly abducted, simply because he uses his technique so unerringly.

There is about a ten-year interval between Svendsen's two symphonies. He was 25 years old when he wrote the first, but showed from the very start an astonishing mastery of orchestration. During his stay in Paris, however, he came into closer contact with the orchestral technique of Berlioz, and this, with his growing experience of practical orchestral work, undoubtedly left its mark.

To this we must add the formative influences of his life. Aimar Grönvold writes in *Norwegian Musicians,*

The B flat major symphony shows us a part of Svendsen's life. It appeared in 1876 and was no doubt deeply inspired by the circumstances under which he lived in those years. It describes, movement by movement, the story of an artist's life in Norway, not always merry, but by no means entirely despondent either. It is freely sprinkled with gloomy passages, which in the Andante swell to a strong lyrical outbrust, unequalled in the modern symphony.

In contrast to this, we can read in *The History of Norwegian Music* (1921) by Gerhard Schjelderup (see next chapter):

I can find nothing profoundly tragic in this symphony. Admittedly we come across certain melancholy passages, but even here vigour and joie de vivre predominate. The themes are clear and light, the composition masterly, and the orchestration unusually melodious . . . artistically this symphony stands even higher than the first, and reveals Svendsen's genius in its fullest flower.

In this short appreciation Schjelderup has summarized the essential features of Svendsen's works, features which recur in the often played compositions such as the Norwegian Rhapsodies, the Festival Polonaise and the other Polonaise in D major, the *Norwegian Artists' Carnival* and *Carnival in Paris.* The two last-named are just as much concert pieces as symphonic pictures, while the fantasy *Romeo and Juliet* and the legend *Zorahayda* are more in the nature of programme music. Johan Svendsen also made a great reputation as a conductor. His talents in this field were so outstanding that the slender opportunities then open to him in his homeland soon proved incapable of holding him. For some years (1872–7 and 1880–3) he led the orchestra of the Christiania Musical Society, which Grieg and other music-lovers had founded in 1871, but during this time he also enjoyed great success as a conductor in various parts of Europe. And when in 1883 he was offered the post of Director of Music at the Royal Theatre in Copenhagen—the Danish capital's operatic stage—he found it hard to refuse.

Thus he came to spend the last part of his life in Denmark. His ceaseless activity as an executant musician and a succession of concert tours to almost every capital in Europe are to some extent at least responsible for the partial eclipse of Svendsen the composer. But it was probably also due to the feeling of restlessness which living abroad inevitably brought on. His love for his native land was manifest in his steadfast resolve to remain a Norwegian subject—even though this meant forfeiting a pension when he resigned from the Theatre in 1908. To make up for this, however, the position he had won, and the esteem he enjoyed found concrete expression in a special grant made by the Danish state in recognition of his services.

Johan Svendsen was a personal friend of Wagner and of Liszt, but as a composer he develops rather the Mendelssohn-Schumann-Gade line in Norway. It was *Johan Selmer,* four years his junior, who was the champion of the symphonic poem in Norway, and, in conjunction with it, of the Wagnerian 'mass orchestra'. The somewhat younger composer Hjalmar Borgström (see next chapter) writes the following note on Selmer:

Not everyone who reckons to have an ear for music will appreciate the importance of Johan Selmer's work as an artist. He has not catered for those content to listen to his music with the outer ear alone. He also demands a receptive inner ear to transmit his notes into the inmost chamber of the mind. Those who prefer the intoxication of beauty for beauty's sake and delight in sounds that are pleasant to the ear will find Johan Selmer somewhat unsatisfying. But he does make an appeal to the ear, for he was too much of an artist to waste his time on arid speculation. The warm blood of life coloured his thoughts, giving them a sensibility that no true art can do without.

But important as this may be, it is not Johan Selmer's major contribution, which is to be found in his very attitude to and conception of music, an attitude so entirely different from that of his Norwegian contemporaries. He was the first Norwegian to realize that music can be the medium for the expression of independent speech and can utter men's thoughts, and that its true artistic worth is dependent on its store of ideas and not on mathematical and arbitrary aesthetic formulas.

It was the music of Berlioz, which Selmer in his youth came to know in Paris, that guided him on his future way. This is seen both in his colourful orchestration and his literary method of composition. The chief works from the pen of Selmer, writer of symphonic poems, are, in chronological order, *Scène funèbre,* where he records impressions of the War of 1870—1, which he experienced in Paris. *The Turks Marching on Athens,* a remarkably realistic picture of the motley Eastern world and of the din of battle in which he introduced certain percussion instruments which had not hitherto been used in a symphony orchestra. Then there was *Carnival in Flanders,* dedicated to 'the master of colour, the painter Fritz Thaulow', itself a remarkably colourful work. And lastly the great tone poem *Prometheus,* where Selmer clearly foreshadows the works of later masters of descriptive music, such as Richard Strauss and Gustav Mahler.

It is owing to the complex instrumentation that these works of Selmer are so seldom performed. It is for his songs, for solo and choir, that Selmer's name is best known in Norway today. They are remarkable for their sensitive and detailed pointing of the text and for their vigorous writing. 'Tollekniven', to words by Chr. Winther, and the songs for choir 'Ulabrand' and 'Norway, Norway' deserve special mention.

Aimar Grönvold says of them: 'One is not much like another, and all of them are unlike any other songs. They are by no means all beautiful, but some are really exquisite.' Selmer himself has declared: 'In the service of poetry I am ruthless, casting rule and tradition overboard. I never strive for an artificial combination: it comes of itself.'

Johan Svendsen, painting by Astri Welhaven   Photo: Norsk Komponistforening

Agathe Backer-Gröndahl
Photo: Norsk Musikforlag

In this generation, Norway produced her first important woman composer, *Agathe Backer Gröndahl*. Though she displayed strength and breadth, boldness and initiative in her work, not least in her piano compositions, it is for her charming lyrics that we best remember her.

She was herself an eminent pianist. Bernard Shaw, in *London Music* (1888—9) calls her 'one of the greatest pianists in Europe. . . . A great artist . . . a serious artist . . . a beautiful, incomparable, unique artist.'

For the piano she wrote a number of delicately poetic character studies, some impressive and beautiful concert studies, as well as arrangements of folk-music. But today she lives rather in her songs, where the spirit and art of poetry have found musical expression of genuine inspiration.

Her work shows a rich melodic vein, as well as the gift of clothing her melodies in a piano accompaniment that carries them on and evokes the mood to perfection. These noble songs are closely related to the romantic lieder of Mendelssohn or Schubert, and some of them—it is enough to mention 'Mot Kveld' ('Eventide')—are enshrined in the hearts of her countrymen just as the songs of Grieg are.

Svendsen, Johan Severin (1840—1911). Born Oslo. At 5 Svendsen received first music lessons from his father, a military band player. Joined a military band, playing several instruments. First composition lessons from Carl Arnold in Oslo. Received scholarship from Carl XV and studied in Leipzig 1864—7, where he wrote first symphony and other major works. Later toured Europe as conductor. 1872—3 Resident conductor Oslo Music Society. 1883—1908 Director of Music, Royal Theatre, Copenhagen. Compositions: 2 symphonies, and *Carnival in Paris, Zorahayda, Norsk Kunstner Karneval,* Romance for violin and orchestra, *Romeo and Juliet,* 4 Norwegian Rhapsodies, all for orchestra. Chamber music including octet and quintet for strings. *Festival polonaise.*

Selmer, Johan Peter (1844—1910). Law studies interrupted by sickness, Selmer turned to music. Studied in Oslo under J. G. Conradi, in Paris under A. Chauver and A. Thomas, in Leipzig under Richter. Conductor, Oslo Music Society 1883—6. Later conducted own compositions in various European towns. For health reasons spent much time in S. Europe in later years. Compositions: *Karneval i Flandern, Scène Funèbre, Prometheus, La marche des Turcs sur Athènes* (chorus and orchestra), *La Captive* (solo and orchestra), also choral works and romances with piano accompaniment.

Gröndahl, Agathe Backer (1847—1907). First music lessons Oslo from O. Winter-Hjelm, H. Kjerulf and L. M. Lindeman. Later studies in Berlin (T. Kullak), Florence (von Bülow), Weimar (Liszt). Later lived mainly in Oslo, but gave concerts in most European countries. Compositions: piano works, songs for piano, piano arrangements of Norwegian folk-tunes.

CHAPTER FOUR

THE INHERITORS

We have already mentioned in passing that the age of Grieg and Svendsen can be called the Golden Age of Norwegian Music. It is not on grounds of quality alone that such a term is justified. A solid phalanx of gifted and skilled composers marches close behind the two leaders. Each has his own special features, but in retrospect, their common characteristics appear most striking—their romantic ideals and the musical forms of expression which were the child of that epoch. The markedly national romanticism typified by Grieg gives way to a romanticism that is more generally European.

The composer David Monrad Johansen (q.v.) has written this account (in *The History of Norwegian Music,* 1921).

Far up in the lonely valleys and isolated hamlets, where the great mountains restrict the view and cast shadows on the mind, where a cheerful lust for life often goes hand in hand with a brooding, introspective yearning, is the home of our folk-music. Small wonder that our composers, too, found a spiritual dwelling in these regions, and that their music took colour and shape from a soil that concealed a great mysterious treasure, our characteristic peasant culture in all its variety. But a rebellious spirit arose, who found no peace in this enchanted fairyland in the mountains, a man of indomitable courage and will, who wished to attempt the stupendous task of breaking down all barriers, levelling the mountains, bursting asunder the enclosed valleys, heading down the fjords, out into the wide untrammelled sea, so that there would be space, broad open country where the sun could shed unhindered the light of day, and the winds blow fresh and strong, where steep waves could dash the spray in one's face, and ponderous breakers thunder against an immovable shore.

In these words Monrad Johansen describes the swing over to what could be called realistic romanticism, for music is still romantic in its tone language. *Christian Sinding*, the leading figure in this movement, and one whose influence was also felt abroad, is described just as unerringly and vividly.

Christian Sinding is above all a spirit of daylight, a fighter, a man of action. Only when he is steering his craft through a troubled sea, when the winds are howling and waves are crashing down, when danger threatens, is he in his right element. No wonder that he has to raise his voice to overcome the tempest—the tempest in his soul. But when the storm is over, and the sun sets, and the long shadows fall across the sea, when the stars one after another come out in the blue sky, this voice takes on a different tone, tender and intimate, yet as manly as before. Then he tells of all life's happenings, great and small, that have moved his soul and touched his heart.

There is another side of Sinding that we must touch on—because it is not without significance. There was a time in the story of man when the word 'chivalry' was in use, but that was long ago and the knights are long dead. Yet their spirit lives on, and shines brightly in Christian Sinding, pervading all his works large or small.

Today we know best the Sinding who "when the storm is over, tells of all life's happenings". He is remarkably resourceful and versatile, giving us opera, cantatas, symphonies, concertos and all kinds of chamber music, and a whole store of piano pieces and romances; and it is these last that are now most frequently heard in the home and the concert hall.

From the very first Sinding made it clear that he was moving in the direction of the main accepted forms. In the years between 1875 and 1880 he wrote a piano concerto and a quartet for strings, which were both performed in Christiania, and both burned afterwards, an event which was frequently repeated whenever the composer, in a mood of self-criticism, revised his manuscripts. Even as late as the nineteen-thirties he wrote: "As the years go by so much rubbish accumulates that it must be burnt to clear the air."

In the decade 1880—90 his great works began to appear, introduced by the piano quintet 1882—84. It was first performed in Oslo in 1885, and three years later in Leipzig.

In this work Sinding evinces a clearly personal style, so much his own that Tchaikovsky, when looking over the manuscript with a mutual friend, made a number of corrections where he thought he detected some obvious slips of the pen. When he learned that this was not the case, he burst out, 'I have taken many liberties in my time but never as many as this!' No wonder then, that opinion was divided on this work when it was first performed at Leipzig; but when played again soon after, it was

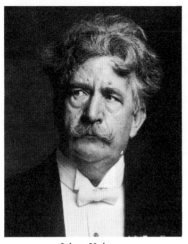

<table>
<tr><td>*Johan Halvorsen*</td><td>*Christian Sinding*</td></tr>
<tr><td>Photo: Norsk Komponistforening</td><td>Photo: Norsk Musikforlag</td></tr>
</table>

Johan Halvorsen
Photo: Norsk Komponistforening

Christian Sinding
Photo: Norsk Musikforlag

universally acclaimed. Today it is undoubtedly one of his works in the larger format which still delights us most.

It was closely followed by the Piano Concerto in D flat major, the First Symphony, and the great choral work, the music for Björnson's *Til Molde*. Of the symphony, Grieg writes: "The other day he played me the first movement of a symphony. It was magnificent. It was in the spirit of the first movement of the Ninth, yet it was all Sinding, not Beethoven."

This letter was written from Leipzig, where Grieg met Sinding and Johan Halvorsen (q.v.) in 1887. He also writes of another of Sinding's works, the *Suite i gammel stil* for two violins: "Sinding and Halvorsen played a suite of Sinding's 'in the old style', that is à la Bach, so deep and full and rich, and so imbued with the spirit of that time, that I do not hesitate to call it a masterpiece."

There are two essential features of Sinding's artistry which attracted Grieg. His breadth and power as a symphonic composer, and his interest in the old set forms of music, forms to which he often reverted, taking dance forms like the minuet, gavotte, and such, and adapting them to his own tonal language, or borrowing from the actual structure of the music of that time.

His development in this direction is not unlike that of Brahms.

But in his orchestration Sinding was much more strongly influenced by Wagner, and it may well be that the somewhat striking harmonic resemblance has to a certain extent weakened the effect of the greater orchestral works—the three symphonies, the piano concerto and the three concertos for violin and orchestra—and this may be why they are so seldom found in the programmes of symphony concerts today.

The numerous piano works strike one at once as fresh, almost impromptu in style. The sparkling gaiety familiar to us from his most famous piano work—*The Rustle of Spring*—is repeated in other pieces; and we find, too, the virile and the chivalrous strain recurring. When his mood becomes more intimate it is seldom touched by hopeless sorrow or despair. The positive and optimistic power breaks through, so that we find a mood of intimate and tender sentiment tempered maybe with a touch of melancholy.

The tone of the many romances he has composed bears much the same stamp, and in the piano compositions we find the same bold outspoken movements where full chord and rolling arpeggio are far more prominent than meticulous brushwork and the linear movement technique. But, as is clearly demonstrated by his works in the larger format—not least the piano quintet—he had no difficulty with this technique, and could even exploit it with great originality and talent.

Among the composers grouped around Grieg and Svendsen (i.e.what we might call the 1840 generation), we have had to confine ourselves to the most significant names, omitting some of those who, in scattered works, still live on in Norwegian music, though to a humbler degree. Such, for example, is *Ole Olsen* (1850—1927), who has an obvious place among our national romanticists. A most active and prominent figure in Norwegian musical circles right up to the time of his death, his name will live long among his countrymen through his *Solefaldsang, Petite Suite* for piano and strings, and a number of choral works.

Of equal importance is *Johannes Haarklou,* born 1847 in the western part of Norway. He grew up in a family with deep roots in the traditions of folk-music, took his musical education first as an organist then as a composer, studying with the leading teachers of Leipzig for several years. Today his choral songs first come to mind ('Varde', 'Fenrir', 'Tord Foleson') but on his list of works we find four symphonies, five operas, concertos for violin and for piano, and a great number of works for organ, oratorios, etc. Haarklou died in 1925.

When we come to Sinding's contemporaries, and those immediate successors who (in their attitude to music) follow the line now laid down, the problem of whom to mention and whom to leave out becomes still more difficult. In a publication of this nature the decisive factor cannot be *how much* their music is still played in Norway. The interest that may be shown in a composer abroad and his contribution to the general development of Norwegian music are just as important.

A good example: *Iver Holter* (1850—1941), who has both an opera, symphony, violon concerto and a good number of well written chamber music on his list of works. Today, though, they are not frequently performed, and his name is more often remembered for what he did as conductor, administrator and teacher of music.

In *Catharinus Elling,* we have a musician who is in many respects like L. M. Lindeman. He was equally well grounded in musical theory and had a profound respect for the classical ideals of European music. His career as a musician was, to start with, similar to Sinding's. He developed an interest in the major forms of composition, and the courage to tackle them; his compositions in strict forms belong, like those of Sinding, to the international neo-classical school. But the greatest debt owed by Norwegian music to Catharinus Elling is without doubt the patient work of research and editing he carried out in the field of folk-music. He collected something like 1,500 melodies and arranged them with great discretion. Apart from his musical education he had a University degree in languages which stood him in good stead in his research work. His critical appreciations in a number of works on Norwegian folk-music are of great value for their careful thought and personal approach. His extensive knowledge of Norwegian folk-music gave a special colour to the songs he himself composed, some two hundred in

44

number, both solos with piano accompaniment, and songs for choirs. They are genuine and graceful in their presentation of mood, simple and free from all grandiloquence.

From time to time his other works, violin compositions, or the major *King Inge and Gregorius Dagsson* for solo voices, chorus and orchestra are still performed, but more frequently we hear his songs and arrangements of folk-tunes.

While Catharinus Elling can to some extent be compared to L. M. Lindeman, an even more striking similarity, both in personal traits and career, exists between *Johan Halvorsen* and Johan Svendsen.

Each played the violin as his principal instrument, and each acquired a thorough working knowledge of the other orchestral instruments from childhood. Like Svendsen, Johan Halvorsen started in a military band in his teens, and was a member of a theatre orchestra at the same age; he developed his own vivid musical qualities along with the standard education in the art. He had the same tireless energy, the same determination to travel abroad and learn. In 1888 we find him as leader in the Philharmonic Society in Aberdeen, and the following year he is in Helsinki, giving concerts, teaching at the Conservatory and making regular journeys, meanwhile, to St. Petersburg for advanced study of the violin under Leopold Auer. In Helsinki, too, he wrote his earliest compositions, the best known of which is the arrangement for strings of the Norwegian folk-song *Rabna-brudlaup uti Kråkjalund*.

His next post was in Bergen, where, after an educational tour of Central Europe, he became Director of the Theatre Orchestra and a member of the Harmonien Musical Society, one of the very oldest in Europe, from 1893 to 1899. His exceptionally popular and often performed *The March of the Boyars* was written for a performance at the theatre in Bergen, and at one of the violin recitals which he himself gave at that time, his arrangement of Handel's Passacaglia for violin and viola was heard for the first time.

From 1899 to the end of his life Johan Halvorsen worked in the capital as conductor of the National Theatre orchestra, building up the orchestra from scratch and composing over a period of time a wide range of excellent theatrical music for various stage performances. These works are a notable proof of Halvorsen's special talent: in them are seen his fertile imagination in harmony, his ability and resourcefulness in adapting himself to many varying styles and alien settings without forfeiting his own personal touch. As a result his work never degenerates into mere stylistic imitation.

The most charming example is undoubtedly his *Bergensiana,* rococo variations on the theme of the Bergen Song, or perhaps the *Suite Ancienne* dedicated to Holberg and written for a performance in Holberg's honour in 1902. For similar occasions he wrote a number of works—his *Hanedans* for *Mascarade* is very popular. But on the whole selecting separate compositions is an unnecessary waste of time, for all he wrote is felicitous, vigorous and genuine, whether composed for an Indian play or an old Norwegian subject like *Fossegrimen*—where he writes for Norway's national instrument the Hardanger fiddle.

It was not only as a violinist that Halvorsen showed an interest in the Hardanger fiddle and the peasant airs *(slåtter)*; he was spiritually as closely related to Grieg as he was to Svendsen. (He was in fact related to Grieg by marriage.)

Halvorsen took a lively interest in Norwegian folk-music. It colours the themes in his classical works—not only in the three Norwegian Rhapsodies. This interest is also apparent in his direct work on the subject. In 1901, at Grieg's request, he noted down a series of airs *(slåtter)* which were played for him by the famous fiddler Knut Dale who in turn had his material at first hand from such specialists as Myllarguten, Haavard Giböen and others. It was these airs that Grieg adapted for the piano in his opus 72. In a letter from Troldhaugen dated December 6th, 1901, Grieg expresses his thanks for the airs in these words:

That's what I call a Saturday night, my dear Halvorsen. Outside the south wind is blowing great guns, shaking the house, while the skies pour down a veritable deluge. But all is quiet and cosy in the drawing room. I have just received your airs, and have this minute read them through again, fairly chuckling with pleasure, though mortified and thwarted that I am no fiddler. Just now I feel it would be a crime to arrange the airs for the piano—yet it is a crime that I am sooner or later going to commit. The temptation is too strong.

Halvorsen himself published an arrangement of the airs for solo violin, as well as a five-part edition of Norwegian songs and dances.

In his impressive total of compositions we find three symphonies, the violin concerto, a considerable amount of chamber music and a very great deal besides. In his orchestral work we must admire chiefly the deft and confident instrumentation, especially in all the work he wrote for an orchestra that was never at full strength, but from which nevertheless he managed to draw a resonant full-bodied tone.

Many of his violin compositions, songs and choral works have retained their popularity while the most popular among the orchestral works are the rhapsodies, the *Bergensiana,* the *Suite Ancienne* and others of the compositions we have mentioned above.

Halvorsen's importance as a conductor deserves a special note. Concurrently with his work in the theatre he gave full support to the orchestral life of the capital during the first decade of this century by means of regular performances of symphonic music in the Theatre with a full orchestra, gradually introducing to the public many of the new compositions of the day. He was also Director of Orchestra to the newly founded Philharmonic Society in 1919—20, but returned to the Theatre and continued his work there, work which he had clearly shown no one could tackle half as successfully as himself.

Now we come to the composers born in the period around 1860—80, who in various ways provide an uninterrupted link with those of whom we have written. When these composers were young Grieg and Svendsen were still dominating influences, but as with Sinding, the music of the younger generation was coloured by later trends. If we are looking for a comprehensive *coup d'oeil* of the period immediately before our own the result will be somewhat confusing: there are reactionary and revolutionary tendencies; traditions are preserved and venerated at the same time as new features emerge. Leading composers like Brahms, Liszt and Wagner and later Reger, Richard Strauss and Debussy have their followers in Norway. Some can be called direct disciples, but most appear to reflect certain features of the great masters, just as Sinding's work shows some features of Brahms's technique of construction and certain aspects of Wagnerian orchestration.

Practically all Norwegian composers are at the same time executant musicians, and have often established a reputation in this capacity.

In this book, however, where the aim is to give an account of Norwegian music as it is today, we should concentrate rather on those whose work is most likely to be heard in the future.

Of the 1860 group *Gerhard Schjelderup* developed as a 'musical dramatist'. Though as a pupil of Massenet he had received his training in France, it was the Wagnerian musical drama that influenced him most in his maturer years and remained his constant model. At the time his works were produced there was no regular opera in Norway and it was mainly abroad that he achieved recognition. Of his eight operas only three have been performed in his own country. He has written symphonic poems for orchestra, for example, on the theme of Henrik Ibsen's *Brand*. It was left to *Hjalmar Borgström,* his junior by five years, to carry on Selmer's work as a composer for the concert hall. His best known symphonic poems are *Tanken* (The Thought), with a recitation in the prologue, *Jesus in Gethsemane* and *Hamlet,* in which the solo role of the piano is notable. Borgström also wrote a number of other works, among them a series of delicately composed romances.

Composers of note in the lyrical style are *Per Lasson* (piano pieces and songs), and *Sigurd Lie,* who is known especially for his romances and choral songs such as 'Sne' (Snow) and 'Nyttårslöier' (New Year's Pranks).

With Sigurd Lie we come to the 1870 generation, which includes *Eyvind Alnaes,* a composer with the same robust unsentimental gusto in his music that we find in Sinding; his romance songs especially stand out for their striking melodies and shapely piano accompaniment and are often heard today in the home and the concert hall.

Halfdan Cleve was an eminent pianist, as was his wife Berit, and it was primarily as a composer for the piano that he made

Arne Eggen
Photo: Norsk Telegrambyrå

his mark. Apart from five piano concertos Cleve's works comprise a rich legacy of piano solos, in character and sentiment comparable to Brahms's own piano compositions.

Johan Backer Lunde was also a pianist, but as an executant musician it is perhaps as an accompanist that he left his mark. In the first few decades of this century we find his name on Norwegian concert programmes coupled with those of most of the world's star singers and instrumentalists, while as a matter of course he regularly accompanied Norwegian performers. This intimate contact with leading artists, coupled with his own lyrical flair, no doubt explains why he developed into a composer of romances. Of the many hundreds of songs he has written a good number have achieved widespread popularity for their feeling and beauty of expression, and the finely constructed piano and voice parts.

When asked what composer had influenced him most, *Arne Eggen* answered without a moment's hesitation—Edvard Grieg. A study of Arne Eggen's work as a whole leaves no doubt that he was a convinced adherent to the national trend in Norwegian music. Even his major works, like the splendid *Ciacona* for the

4

organ—also adapted for orchestra—or the sonatas for strings, have a strong Norwegian character, which is even more marked when we come to the songs. Apart from his enthusiasm for Grieg he may well have been influenced by his elder brother, Dr. Erik Eggen, an authority on folk-music, for we find among his work some fine examples of folk-tune arrangements.

Traces of folk-music are also evident in his major works and his choice of subject, too, indicates his leanings. He wrote an important cantata for chorus and orchestra, based on Hulda Garborg's poem *Mjösen,* and he also wrote the music for her play *Liti Kjersti.* Some of the songs from these works are among the best things he has done in folk-music style; they show how simply and naturally the tunes come to him, without straining for effect. They are deservedly among his most popular works, particularly in the form of an orchestral suite adapted from the *Liti Kjersti* music. For the Church Jubilee in 1930 he wrote a large oratorio for solo voices, chorus and orchestra with organ accompaniment, entitled *King Olav.* Here his ability to give vivid dramatic form to the large format, and his rich contrapuntal movement, are in evidence.

Later works have followed along these lines. Arne Eggen in his maturity specialized in major dramatic works. 1940 saw the première of his opera *Olav Liljekrans* at the National Theatre in Oslo. The opera is based on one of Henrik Ibsen's earlier plays, the subject of which is taken from a saga of the Norwegian Middle Ages. Arne Eggen has succeeded in striking a genuine note which is admirably suited to the text, giving the period and the milieu the right musical setting, with no loss of real dramatic power. From this music too, Arne Eggen has adapted a suite for orchestra which is often found in concert programmes.

In 1951 there appeared a new operatic work by Arne Eggen, *Cymbeline,* based on one of Shakespeare's lesser known plays. In *Cymbeline,* the action of which takes place at the very start of the Christian era, there is no notable Norwegian inflexion, but Eggen's familiarity with the archaic side of Norwegian folk-music no doubt stood him in good stead when it came to giving suitable musical colour to his dramatic material.

Arne Eggen has played an important role on the administrative side of Norwegian music. He had a hand in the foundation, in 1928, of TONO, the international copyright bureau which safeguards the rights of Norwegian composers, and was for many years chairman of the Society of Norwegian Composers, of which he is the first honorary president.

A year junior to Eggen we have *Alf Hurum,* who also—at least to some extent—based his work on Norwegian romantic folk-music, but who was gradually more and more influenced by international trends. Hence (with Trygve Torjussen, 1885 –1977) he became representative of impressionism and transferred its idiom to Norwegian music. According to Hurum himself, impressionism did not make a deep mark on his artistic evolution. He looked upon it rather as an experimental stage in his development, and it is true that this is less noticeable in later years: the best-known works of Alf Hurum were all composed before 1920. Among them are quite a number, both songs and piano pieces, which have an established place in the home, while his two sonatas for piano and violin are fairly well known.

NOTES TO CHAPTER FOUR

Sinding, Christian (1856–1941). Early musical training in Oslo (G. Böhn and L. M. Lindeman). Later learned violin and composition in Leipzig and Munich. Later spent summer in Norway and winter in Europe. Compositions include 4 symphonies, piano concerto (D flat major), violin concerto, Rondo infinito for orchestra, various chamber music, piano works and songs with piano accompaniment.

Elling, Catharinus (1858–1942). Musical education Leipzig and Berlin, also took degree in languages. Became music teacher, organist and critic in Oslo. Collected and published large numbers of Norwegian folk-melodies. Compositions include: the opera *The Cossacks,* music for Shakespeare's *Twelfth Night, Emperor and Galilean* (Ibsen), 2 symphonies, Theme and Variations for orchestra, *The Prodigal Son* (oratorio), and various choral works, chamber music, songs for male voice choir and romances.

Halvorsen, Johan (1864–1935). Musical training Stockholm and Leipzig. Later studied violin in St. Petersburg with Leopold Auer, Berlin (A. Becker) and Liège (C. Thomson). Posts as conductor included that at Harmonien in Bergen. Director of Music, National Theatre, Oslo. Compositions: music for plays including *Fossegrimen, Kongen, As You Like It* and *Mascarade.*

Also 3 symphonies and 3 Norwegian Rhapsodies, and the *Entrance March of the Boyars.*

Schjelderup, Gerhard (1859—1933). Musical education in Paris, where his teachers included Massenet. After 1890 lived chiefly in Germany. Became Professor of Music in Munich. Compositions include operas, *Östenfor sol og vestenfor måne, Sonntagsmorgen, Norwegische Hochzeit, Bruderovet, En hellig aften, Stjærnenætter* and others; 2 symphonies; symphonic poems *Brand* and *Prometheus;* chamber music and songs.

Borgström, Hjalmar(1864—1925). Early training Oslo, later Leipzig and Berlin. Became music critic in Oslo. Compositions include 2 symphonies; symphonic poems, *Tanken, Hamlet* and *Jesus i Gethsemane;* operas *Thora* and *Der Fischer:* a piano concerto, cantatas, chamber music, piano works and songs.

Lasson, Per (1859—1883). Pupil of Bredo Lasson and Johan Svendsen. Compositions include—for piano, *Crescendo* and *Une Demande;* various romances with German and Norwegian texts.

Lie, Sigurd (1871—1904). Trained at Oslo Music Conservatory and Leipzig. Became violinist and conductor. Compositions include a number of romances, piano works and compositions for violin and piano; also unpublished, a symphony, a symphonic march and *Oriental Suite.*

Alnaes, Eyvind (1872—1932). Trained at Oslo Music Conservatory and Leipzig. Became organist and music teacher, chiefly in Oslo. Responsible for most of the harmonization of the Norwegian Church chorale book. Compositions include 2 symphonies, symphonic variations for orchestra, a piano concerto, cantatas, piano pieces and romances.

Cleve, Halfdan (1879—1952). Studied with O. Winter-Hjelm in Oslo, later in Berlin. Pianist and music teacher. Compositions include 5 piano concertos, a violin sonata, a piano sonata, a number of minor piano pieces and *Blomster Sange* (Flower Songs) for solo voice and orchestra.

Lunde, Johan Backer (1874—1958). Pupil of Agathe Backer Gröndahl, I. Holter, F. Busoni and H. Urban. Pianist and accompanist. Compositions include a symphony and various minor orchestral works, songs with orchestral piano pieces and a great many romances for voice and piano.

Eggen, Arne (1881—1955). Musical education at Oslo Music Conservatory and in Leipzig. Organist at Tanum Church. Compositions include operas *Olav Liljekrans* and *Cymbeline,* light opera *Liti Kjersti,* oratorio *King Olav,* a symphony, several choral works, *Ciaconna* for organ, arranged also for orchestra, 2 violin sonatas and songs.

Hurum, Alf (1882-1972). Studied in Berlin, Paris and Leningrad. Settled in Hawaii since 1924, where he is conductor and music teacher. Compositions include a symphony, *Bendik and Aarolilja* (symphonic poem), *Exotic Suite for orchestra, Eventyrland* (Fairyland) (suite for orchestra), chamber music and a number of songs and piano pieces.

CHAPTER FIVE

THE PRESENT TIME

In a survey of this kind a title such as "The Present Century" might have been as appropriate as "The Present Time". Even if all the composers mentioned in the previous chapter are now dead, the youngest of them are only a very few years older than some of the composers who will be mentioned in this chapter, and some of these are also dead now. Development in art goes on continuously, so any kind of strict borderline will be equally impossible to draw. My reason for mentioning some of those at the end of Chapter Four was that they may be considered to be more closely bound to tradition in their music than the majority of the composers we are going to deal with in this chapter. However, it is essential to stress the fact that virtually whenever one is tracing artistic and stylistic development, it is impossible to separate one group from another by drawing rigid dividing lines, or to put any single creative artist into a well defined category.

When dealing with those composers we named "the Inheritors" we noticed that two groups emerged at about the end of the 1880s, one consciously adhering to nationalism and the other seeking contact with the more classical line developed in central Europe by composers such as Brahms and Bruckner, while at the same time maintaining their ties with the Norwegian characteristics in the music of their immediate predecessors. All the composers dealt with in the previous chapter were born before 1890. Some of those we are going to mention now belong to the same generation, but most of the composers to be dealt with in this chapter were born after that date.

There will be a few exceptions, and we start with *Fartein Valen* – left on purpose for this chapter because of his unique place in the development of creative Norwegian music.

Fartein Valen was born as early as 1887, but until the outbreak

Fartein Valen   Photo: Norsk Telegrambyrå

of World War II he was the one real modernist among our composers, practically the only one writing dodecaphonic music, which he had been doing since the early twenties.

Like many other great minds, Valen had to fight for recognition almost all his life, for he was so far ahead of other composers.

He himself said, "All the time I knew with a deep inner conviction that I had to write in a different way from composers at that time. I found them weak harmonically: they seemed lifeless." He started in a rich tonal style, modelling himself above all on Brahms and Reger. His harmonic pattern was complex and rich in chromaticism, and at the same time dissonant polyphony played a role of ever-increasing importance. Even at that early stage he was composing "in a different way", but he was constantly struggling. By the year 1921 he had published only four works. His inward struggle went on until that year: gradually he reached the border of tonality, then he had to break through it and join the revolutionaries of that time.

An indication of the extent of this inward struggle is the fact that his Trio, opus 5 (1923) for piano, violin and cello, had been rewritten nine times since he started working on it in 1917. It is in this work that he uses a twelve-tone technique for the first time. The atonal polyphony he develops is decidedly personal, quite different from Schoenberg's. He builds on dissonant relationships between the parts, and allows themes and motifs comparatively free development. His music is not restricted to certain sequences or series, but he uses the system in a free, personal way. Valen's themes often have fewer than twelve notes, and he frequently repeats them. Another striking trait is the brilliant counterpoint with which he knits his melodies together: the themes are interwoven, varied, inverted, split up into motifs, spun out, repeated as canons or cancrizans, in a way parallelled only in the works of the great masters of the Renaissance or Baroque periods. His music is often — and rightly — described as "dissonant polphony". During the years when he was struggling to find his form, he made an intensive study of the counterpoint of Palestrina and the other masters of his time, and when younger composers came to study under him, he advised them to do the same.

Valen's development can be followed step by step, from the swelling chords of late Romanticism to an almost ethereal polyphony. In the course of his development his compositions become more and more linear, and his polyphony takes on an increasingly tenuous quality, acquiring a special airiness and transparency. The latter trend is evident in the Goethe songs, opus 6 and opus 7. In *Suleika* he combines two themes with five motifs in all; on the basis of the motifs he then develops all four parts of the composition in dissonant counterpoint. The contrapuntal lines contain nothing which cannot be derived from the five "basic motifs": these are inserted in turn, are transposed, and appear in contractions and expansions.

This technique was soon developed further through the use of thematic inversions, and the earliest example of this development is heard in his first purely orchestral work. *Pastorale*, opus 11, from 1930. The tendency is even more pronounced in the second String Quartet (1931). During the next ten years, from

1930 to 1940, he wrote a good number of his best-known works: a series of short orchestral pieces, compositions for piano and for organ, and unaccompanied choral works based on texts from the Bible or on hymns by the Nordic writers Kingo, Brorson and Urbimontanus. The sacred pieces reflect the deeply religious quality that pervaded Valen's personality.

The exquisitely poetic concordance with the texts is striking, and shows how strong the urge was for him to wring poetic expression from the new technique, to use it to express his inward feelings and spiritual experiences. The Russian-American pianist Alexandr Helmann, an ardent admirer of Valen who in 1949 took the initiative of founding a Valen Society in Britain, once said of Valen's music, "Most of the composers writing atonal music are still (i.e. about 1950) occupied with the mechanical side of it, but Fartein Valen has mastered this to such a degree that his genius creates real poetry from it."

The titles of many of his shorter orchestral works clearly reveal his urge to express inward feelings: examples are *Sonetto di Michelangelo*, opus 18 (1932), *Epithalamion*, opus 18 (1933) *Le Cimetière Marin*, opus 20 (1934) and *La Isla de las Calmas*, opus 21 (1934).

We can best illustrate how Fartein Valen tried to express himself in compositions of this nature by quoting his own words on *Le Cimetière Marin:*

The inspiration came to me when, during a stay on Majorca, I read a translation of Paul Valéry's famous poem in the Spanish newspaper *El Sol*. '*Le Cimetière Marin* is Paul Valéry's masterpiece,' says the foreword to the translation. It is a philosophical meditation, in the manner of Parmenides and Zenon, describing life's ephemeral vicissitudes, inspired by the churchyard at Sète. This made me think of another churchyard near my home in western Norway: an old, disused burial ground where cholera victims had once been laid to rest. The music does not follow the poem programatically, but seeks to voice the reflections which arise wherever Man stands face to face with Death.

It was this work which, at the ISCM Festival in Copenhagen in 1947, gained Valen international recognition; this in turn made his own countrymen accept him as one of the leading composers of the time, and from this point onwards it was no longer just a small circle of devoted friends and admirers who recognised his greatness.

When Fartein Valen died in 1952 he had just finished a piano concerto in one movement, and he left sketches for a fifth symphony. Despite the obvious problems involved in using the sonata form when writing atonal, dissonant polyphony, Valen used his adaptation of this form in his symphonies and in other large works: in his violin concerto from 1940, for instance, and in the chamber works.

Valen's struggle in the 1920s and 1930s started as an inner one, but later became a struggle with the world around him as well, a world in which art was still strongly dominated by national romanticists. They may not have been so in the strictly stylistic sense of the term, but they certainly were in their inner attitude, in their unfaltering fidelity to the national idioms. Even if the musical language of these composers is more up to date than that of Romanticism, in most cases it nevertheless has its roots firmly embedded in Norwegian folk music. One reason for this is the dominating influence exerted by a personality like Grieg's. We find the same phenomenon in Finnish music, where the dominating influence is still that of Sibelius. But another reason, just as valid as the first, is the fact that Norway is still so young as a free, independent nation. We are still in a period of national self-assertion, and what happened during and after World War II has further emphasised this trend in Norwegian music.

A representative of this trend is the composer *Arne Eggen*, who was mentioned at the end of the previous chapter. He was at the zenith of his activity as a mature artist in the period 1920–1940, and it was during these years that some of his most important works were written.

We come now to the period leading up to the end of the 1950s, and from now onwards composers will not be mentioned in chronological order, but will be examined as representatives of one of the following four groups: declared nationalists, "hybrids", moderate modernists, and futurists and avant-gardists.

Sparre Olsen
Photo: Norsk Telegrambyrå

David Monrad Johansen
Photo: Norsk Musikkinformasjon

The leaders of the first group were Arne Eggen and his junior by one year, *David Monrad Johansen* (born 1888). Probably no other Norwegian composer of our time has followed more wholeheartedly in Grieg's footsteps in his treatment of our folk music than has Monrad Johansen. But side by side with Grieg's influence we find idioms similar to those of French Impressionism, and Monrad Johansen himself has recognised this influence on his music. But it is the Impressionists' harmonies and the inner structure of their music, rather than form and style, which live on in his earlier works. He used the wider tonal range which Impressionism gave him, to clothe the Norwegian melodies with a richer and more original harmony than they would otherwise have. In a way there is a curious cycle involved here, for on their own admission the Impressionists were inspired by the harmonies which Grieg evolved when adapting the harmonic tones of Romanticism to the demands of Norwegian melody.

Monrad Johansen is one of the greatest experts on Greig's music, a fact that is made gloriously clear by the great Grieg biography he wrote in 1934. His profound sympathy with native music characterises his piano suites, which are based on Dr. O. M. Sandvik's collection of Gudbrandsdal music, and is equally evident in both the Sonata for Violin and Piano (1912) and the "Norse Oratorio" *Voluspå* (1927), the work which, together with his composition on the medieval ballad *Draumkvæde* and the song-cycle *Nordlands Trompet*, assured him his place in Norwegian musical history.

By simple, forceful means and a lapidary style, he brings to life dramatic stories from our Old Norse sagas, from medieval epic poetry and from the works of the poet Peter Dass (1647–1707).

For many years Monrad Johansen wrote in a simple homophonic style, using melodies imbued with the spirit of folk music and harmonies organically adapted to them. Only in his later years do we find leanings towards polyphony, the first work in a more intricate contrapuntal form being the University Cantata *Ignis Ardens* (1931).

In 1939 Monrad Johansen was commissioned by the Norwegian Broadcasting Corporation to write a symphonic poem, *Pan*, for the celebration of Knut Hamsun's eightieth birthday. This is probably his most frequently performed work, and marks a balance between his earlier style, with traces of impressionistic colouring, and a more elaborate contrapuntal style. The work is a splendid tribute to the poet who had, in the genius of his younger days, revealed a new world of natural mysticism and shown its forces at work in men's minds. The countryside of northern Norway comes to life in both the poetry and the music: Monrad Johansen, like Hamsun, had spent his childhood in northern Norway.

A few years before writing *Pan*, Monrad Johansen went to Professor Grabner in Leipzig, prompted by a strongly-felt need to deepen his knowledge of specific aspects of composition in order to follow current developments on the general European musical scene more closely. The first result of this visit was the *Symphonic Phantasy* of 1936. In his mature style, which may be said to start with this work, it is not so much actual polyphony which is significant, as the transformation of motifs and themes. The most remarkable of his post-war works are the *Symphonic Variations* (1947), the *Piano Concerto* (1955), the *Flute Quintet* op. 35, composed for the hundredth anniversary of the Norwegian League of Composers (1967), and the *String Quartet* (1969).

As mentioned earlier, David Monrad Johansen was a leader of the nationalistic group in the 1920s. In his works like *Voluspå* and some of his other choral works from that time he was considered to have reached the ideal solution for creating a specifically Norwegian tone language. This found expression mainly in the use of modes which we find in many of our folk tunes, together with a tendency for the parts to run in parallel fifths and fourths. This tends to give the music a somewhat primitive and original stamp, and the results were forthwith labelled Norwegian. In regarding these works as characteristically Norwegian we should not, of course, forget that the church modes were part of the common European heritage of the Middle Ages, and that composers from several other European countries have also used them in more recent times.

It was not long before the use of these elements became unduly rigid in form. The new generation of composers waiting to take over was therefore faced with two problems: their relationship to the music of the day, and their relationship to the national heritage. The men who made their musical debut in the late twenties and early thirties tackled these problems and solved them each in his own way. Most of the composers at that time — the generation born around the turn of the century — had a common aim. They were eager and able to adapt Norwegian folk music in some way or other to their compositions. This striving towards an independent Norwegian style of music may possibly be regarded as an echo from the ideals of the national romantic age. But from the purely musical point of view their efforts can hardly be classed as romantic. The problem facing this generation was how to weave Norwegian strands into the musical idiom of the time. It is according to their degree of "Norwegianism" and radicalism that the presentation of the following composers is arranged.

On the extreme nationalist wing we find *Eivind Groven*. He is the stoutest champion of the view that Norwegian classical music must be based directly on Norwegian folk music. He was born in 1901 in Telemark, and grew up in this district, one of the

Eivind Groven   Photo: Norsk Telegrambyrå

country's richest centres of folk music; it was here he received his lasting impressions. He later went on to compose on the basis of these, and in order to keep his links with folk music fresh and unsullied he would never submit to any other systematic teaching. As a composer he is therefore almost self-taught.

The first striking trait is his skill as a lyricist. The melodies, with their unusual intervals derived from Norwegian folk-music, are tuneful, typical and beautiful, and the harmonies are adjusted and moulded to the melodies with a strong personal touch.

Although Groven's inspiration may come from the world of folk music, and especially from the Hardanger fiddle, on which he was an expert, there is nevertheless no direct borrowing. The features we have mentioned are evident in the composition with which he made his debut, the orchestral suite *Renaissance* (1925), and in two larger works for chorus and orchestra: *Brudgommen* and *Mot Ballade*, both from 1933. Besides these we have a series of excellent songs, both with orchestral and with piano accompaniment, and of choral songs, all infused with a delicate lyrical mood.

In vocal compositions like his *Draumkvede* (one of his later more extensive works) he was able to combine genuine folk song themes with his own melodies, without the combination causing any break in style.

Groven has also taken up more highly developed instrumental forms. He has written two symphonies: the first of them won him first prize in a competition arranged by the Norwegian Broadcasting Corporation in 1937, and the second was composed in 1946. While Groven adheres to the structural principles typical of folk tunes — short periods linked together — it is obvious that he cannot possibly obtain the tension, the dramatic conflict or the contrasts necessary to the construction of really effective symphonic movements. The French conductor Albert Wolff once said of one of the symphonies: "This is not one symphony, but there is material in it for fifty." In the course of time, though, Groven arrived at a more effective solution to these problems, as is demonstrated in his *Piano Concerto* from 1950, and above all in the festival ouverture *Hjalarljod* from the same year.

Groven is also remarkable as a theoritician and organ constructor. In 1927 he wrote a study on the "nature scale", and in 1948 a book entitled *Temperation and Untempered Music*. In the course of a good number of years as an inventor and constructor he has managed to construct an organ with each octave divided into 36 intervals, thus making it possible to produce any kind of modulations based on untempered scales, such as are possible in the tempered scales.

Groven died in 1977.

Although *Sparre Olsen* (born 1903) spent most of his youth in Oslo and Bergen, he has remained a decided nationalist. However, his interpretation follows lines other than those of Groven. His harmony is adapted to Norwegian melodies in an original manner : although some of his chord combinations point back to Grieg, they have a much sterner and more modern quality. Sparre Olsen employs boldly dissonant chord combinations, and takes his time before resolving them. With his soft, pastel shades he achieves a delicate effect, and — like Groven — he has a pronounced lyrical vein. Among his finest works are his songs, both with piano accompaniment and for chorus. All through his creative life he has demonstrated his fine lyric talent in a very large number of songs. Some of them are to be found in various arrangements, for example for different kinds of choirs or transcribed for different instruments, due to the fact that they have attained such extensive popularity. His best-known work is probably the choral song *Fjell-Norig* (Norway of the Mountains), almost a national song today, with the character of a folk tune, in as far as thousands of people undoubtedly sing it without realizing that it is a song written by a man still living amongst us today.

In the mid-1920s Sparre Olsen studied in Germany for several years, and is fully familiar with composers like Hindemith and Bartók. He has made a thorough study of techniques of the European composers of today, and has practised them. But the things that lie closest to his heart, the elements that have formed and that continue to imbue his personality, are Norwegian folk music as he himself has absorbed it, Norwegian folklore in all its manifestations, Norwegian landscape, and Norwegian poetry.

Sparre Olsen has devoted most of his attention to the smaller forms. His suites for piano *From Telemark* and *Leitom Suite* belong to his earlier years, but also among the works from later years are a good number of various samples of his lyric vein, such as "Twilight Tunes" op. 64 for solo horn, *Aubade,* and *Nocturne* op. 57 for flute and horn. Nevertheless, through the years he has also composed more extensive works, among them an oratorio for choir, recitation and orchestra on the *Draumkvæde,* a great visionary poem from the Middle Ages (1937), *Symphonic Phantasy* (1938/39), *Nidarosdomen* – a fugue and choral – (1947), *Music for Orchestra* (1948) and *Pastorale and Dance* (1949). In these works we notice his sure sense of detail and symmetry and his ease in polyphonic construction. Sensitivity, clarity and balance are the hallmarks of Sparre Olsen's works. This is not least remarkable in his second *Symphonic Phantasy* from 1957. Among his later works is also a third *Symphonic Phantasy,* on a folktune from northern Norway, his op. 56.

Also chamber music in many different combinations has appeared throughout his life: there is a string quartet, op. 55,

Dialogues for flute and viola, op. 50, a wind quintet, and several works where the horn plays an important part. This is not least the case in one of his most recent works, a *Concertino* for horn and string orchestra. Most popular among his orchestral works is probably his stage music for Tore Ørjasæters *Anne på Torp,* which is frequently performed as an orchestral suite.

Another talented and prolific composer among the nationalists is *Geirr Tveitt* (1908–1980). From his native Hardanger Geirr Tveitt had wide and most fantastic visions of the monumentality of a genuine Norse music. Ever since he made his debut in Norwegian music with his *Tvorøystes Fyrestudier* (two-part inventions in Lydian, Phrygian and Dorian modes) he has been a sworn adherent to the Norwegian line. In the pre-war years his ardent nationalism led to a number of excesses: the ballet *Baldurs Draumar,* written for an orchestra of 100 players and 9 pentatonically tuned Stone Age drums, another great ballet *Birgingu* and the opera *Dragaredokko* in 5 acts, both based on ancient saga material. He set out the theoretical basis of his compositions in a controversial treatise, *Tonalität-Theorie des Parallelen Leittonsystems* (1937), where he claims that the modal scales which occur in folk music constitute an independent Norwegian system, and for the commonly accepted terms Dorian, Phrygian etc. he substitutes names of old Norse modes (rir-sum-fum-tyr). These words come from Hávámál's 161st strophe, which deals with the origin of music. The book is a gigantic effort to elaborate a special functional theory on the basis of an *a priori* basic tone conception for these scales, and throws interesting light on Tveitt's own technique of composition.

Nevertheless, his solid knowledge of international development in music during his lifetime led him to integrate in a natural way traits like the use of clusters and similar effects in some of his later works.

The years since the war seem to have brought more clarity and balance into his production. He has displayed a high degree of skill in instrumentation, not least in the *Hundrad Hardingtonar,* 100 folk tunes from Hardanger, adapted and interpreted with great originality. Stravinsky and some other typical colourists may come to mind when one listens to these compositions, but to a Norwegian mind they appeal above all through the homogeneity of the original tune (which he never alters) and the colourful draping Tveitt has given it, always giving a precise characteristic of the content or background of the tune. Besides these Hardanger-tonar — surely his most frequently performed opus, consisting of several suites, each of about 15 numbers — we should also mention his *piano sonatas* (at least 29 of them) his *piano concertos* (5–6) and *two concertos for Hardanger fiddle* with symphony orchestra, the second of which is an example of programmatic music, as the movements, in accordance with the titles, depict three of the largest Norwegian fjords. (If the number of sonatas and piano concertos is given inaccurately, the reason is that a disastrous fire completely burnt down his home in Hardanger, where all his manuscripts were kept.)

Tveitt's most important work from recent years is the opera *Jeppe,* based on Ludvig Holberg's comedy. It was composed in 1964–65, but thoroughly revised and reorchestrated in 1967–68. This work was commissioned by the Bergen Festival and had its world premiere there. Since then it has also been performed at the Norwegian State Opera in Oslo.

Before turning to some important composers of the second category, belonging to the same generation as David Monrad Johansen, it is appropriate to mention here one or two other composers, even one younger than those mentioned previously, since ideologically and idiomatically they are declared nationalists.

Marius Moaritz Ulfrstad (1890–1968) entered the Musikhochschule in Berlin after studying in Oslo, and later he was also a pupil of Respighi, Pizetti and Ravel. Abroad he assimilated the techniques of modern composition, and on his return home he set himself the task of giving expression to the varied and vivid life of his compatriots, using Norwegian idioms combined with dramatic energy. He has left 5 symphonies and several chamber works, the titles of which indicate their national character. His music for the theatre, major works for choir and orchestra, such as *Arnljot Gelline, Lex Imperat* (Nidaros Choral Symphony), his suites for orchestra (the Arctic, the Svalbard, the Greenland and the Scandia) as well as his songs, have all been received with interest when performed. His music for Knut Hamsun's "Munken Vendt" was commissioned by the Vienna Burgtheater, but also performed at the Schiller Theatre, Berlin.

Olav Kielland (born 1901) is a declared champion of native elements in music. After active years as a conductor of the Philharmonic Society in Oslo he retired at the end of World War II to Telemark. He has been living there since then, associating with players of the Hardingfele, studying their technique and absorbing many elements of this into his own composing. Thoroughly familiar with symphonic forms and the handling of themes, he has in an admirable way shown his ability to combine the typical Norwegian elements with these in his *Concerto Grosso Norvegese* from 1951–52. Going back to his earlier years we should mention his *Suite per Orchestra,* op. 5, from 1939, honoured with prizes from the Norwegian Broadcasting Corporation and the League of Composers. Often performed is his *Marcia Nostrale,* op. 11, also for orchestra, as well as his 20 piano pieces, op. 13, edited under the title *Villarkorn* (something which may be described as magic charm which causes one to go astray or lose one's memory).

Kielland has mostly devoted his compositions to the orchestra: there are, for example, two symphonies, of which the second, from 1961, his op. 21, won the prize of Musikselskabet Harmonien, Bergen, in the same year. There is a *Violin Concerto,* op. 7, the *Overtura Tragica* for Ibsen's "Brand", and for song and orchestra the symphonic suite *Mot Blåsnøhøgdom* and *Sivle-songar* (poems by Per Sivle). In most of these works we find polyphony with dissonant lines. Kielland has also written compositions for String Quartet, his op. 22 from 1964, as well as songs for male choir.

Øistein Sommerfeldt (born 1919) belongs to the younger generation of composers. He keeps to the free tonal style, he says, because in this way he can maintain a connection with simple melodic revelation such as it comes to life through the folk tune. Yet there is, in some works, more tonal freedom, sometimes giving examples of sporadic polytonality or even approaching the borderline of atonality. He has composed a good number of songs, piano pieces, some chamber music and orchestral works.

Ludvig Irgens Jensen   Photo: Norsk Telegrambyrå

Most important among the works for orchestra are a *Small Ouverture* and his *First Symphony,* named *La Betulla,* on which he worked for several years around 1970, revising it finally in 1973.

The 1970s were for Øistein Sommerfeldt highly productive years in which he both created new works and at the same time revised several of his more important earlier ones such as his *Suite No. 1 for Orchestra,* based on Grieg's "Slåtter". For the celebration of the eleven-hundredth anniversary of Norway's union under one king he composed *Hafrsfjord,* for recitation and orchestra (1972). Several works have been commissioned by Norwegian television.

Generally we may say that in his work he has shown his capability of forming his intentions in a musical language that is part of the unbroken prolongation of the structural symphonic line which starts with Svendsen and continues up to Irgens Jensen.

And so this seems to be the right place to turn to *Ludvig Irgens Jensen* (1894–1969). He has often been called "the humanist" among contemporary composers in Norway. He has shown a peculiar talent for composing without relying on current fashions, yet without appearing to be a reactionary. His works have a personal touch, a deep quality that derives from a strong fund of experience, yet at the same time they possess a clear, concise form, and a content of purely classical character. He started as a lyricist, with the song cycle *Japanischer Frühling* to poems by Hans Bethge, and six other opuses with all in all 38 songs; all these works appeared in the year 1920. There are obvious similarities with the tone-colour style of Monrad Johansen from the same time, and both composers were to some extent inspired by Impressionism. But in the case of Irgens Jensen there are also contrapuntal elements which point forward to his further development.

We note these qualities in the massive orchestral work *Passacaglia* (1926). This composition, which won a prize in the international competition organized in connection with the Schubert Centenary in 1928, shows us a composer who seeks to fuse polyphony with a simple natural development of melody, which is set against a richly coloured background. The composition consists of four main parts: an introduction presenting a series of themes, which are not fully developed until later in the work; a passacaglia movement consisting of the theme with twelve variations; a most dramatic and tumultuous triple fugue; and finally another passacaglia movement which connects and sums up most of the themes treated in the earlier movements. In at least one of the themes we can notice a flavour of folk music. This Norwegian flavour was more strongly in evidence in his compositions from the 1930s, especially in the oratorio — or "dramatic symphony" as its sub-title reads — *Heimferd*.

This was written for the St. Olav Jubilee in Trondheim in 1930. In it can be traced influences from sacred music and Norwegian folk music. In one place the composer has even had the Hardanger fiddle in mind, viz. in the fifth movement, where a solo violin symbolizes King Olav's homecoming with light *slåtte* rhythms. But the composer never borrows directly from folk music; he rather suggests its mood and atmosphere with typical phrases and chords. The same can be said of his *Partita Sinfonica* (1939), a suite from the music to Kinck's play "Driftekaren". In

1942 Irgens Jensen completed a Symphony in two movements, which won the first prize in a competition in connection with the Norwegian Composers' League's 25th anniversary in 1943. Another first prize was bestowed upon him in the competition in connection with the 900th anniversary of Oslo for his festival overture "Canto d'omaggio", in 1949.

In these works we find the Norwegian sense of melody together with an elaborate contrapuntal arrangement, logical construction and an artistic form comparable with that of the Baroque era. The range is wide, from lyrical moods inspired by nature to a questing meditation which at times gives the music a brooding "philosophizing" air. It seems that variations were Ludvig Irgens Jensen's favourite medium for attaining his greatest effects.

In the minor musical forms Irgens Jensen has produced some delicate, finely balanced and carefully executed works. A number of songs for piano accompaniment reveal the depth of his nature, and so do some of his choral songs, strong in line and melody, at the same time emphasizing the nuances in the text with supple fluency.

Ludvig Irgens Jensen is a natural link with, and to a great extent an exponent for, the larger school of Norwegian composers whose aim is to combine essentially Norwegian features with the musical idiom of the day. I labelled them previously "the Hybrids" — without any derogatory intention! — since they are consciously national-cum-radical, and according to the manner in which each of these composers emphasizes the "Norwegian" or the "modernistic" elements, so we meet a series of individual solutions to the problem of modern Norwegian music versus the general European trend.

Bjarne Brustad (born 1895) is in his art a kind of common denominator for these tendencies. He aims to be both Norwegian and European in his production, deliberately seeking to combine nationalistic and modern elements in his music. He was, like Monrad Johansen and Irgens Jensen, first influenced by the Impressionists and later by the more modern French composers, like Milhaud and Honegger. His contact with these composers

Bjarne Brustad

Photo: Norsk Telegrambyrå

evoked his daring and complicated rhythms and his radical use of bitonal and polytonal effects. In 1934 he came into closer contact with Bartók, and this confirmed his inclination to continue trying to solve the problem of uniting the Norwegian traits with modern composition technique. He develops a harmonic style without cadence, often with bitonal interchange of parts. Contrasts and change are effected by setting against each other blocks of varying size and kind. The motifs may move against a background of sustained dissonances, they may be brought together by parallel chords, or appear in passages of pure consonance.

By 1930 he had found his own personal mode of expression. In his further development his attempt to unite national and modern characteristics in his music is not very apparent. This we see in the works of his later period, which include his 9 symphonies.

As principal teacher of composition at the Conservatory of Music in Oslo for more than 25 years, Bjarne Brustad has been playing a major role in determining trends for the next generation of Norwegian composers. There are few composers of note who have not studied composition, and above all orchestration, under his guidance. Through his thorough studies as well as through his work in and with orchestras for many years he has been generally considered as the leading authority in this field. He is also the author of a book on musical composition, as well as a handbook on fundamental violin technique.

The list of Brustad's compositions contains all sorts of instrumental music, symphonic music and chamber music for the theatre, also opera, songs and several arrangements of Norwegian folk music. Being a severe self-critic, Brustad has in the course of the years rejected and destroyed a good number of compositions. His leading works are *Caprice for violin and viola* (1932), *Concertino for Viola and Chamber Orchestra* (1932), *Rhapsody for Violin and Orchestra* (1933), *Kinderspiele — From a Child's Life —* for piano (1934), orchestrated (1956), *Sonata no. 1 for Violin* (1935), *Concerto Grosso* (1938), *Trio for Clarinet, Violin and Viola* (1938).

During the Second World War no works appeared, but since 1945 a long series of important compositions confirms that his creative power had maintained its force up to his later years. Between 1948 and 1973 he composed *9 symphonies,* the last four during the period 1970–73, and four *Concertos for Violin and Orchestra.* Other works from his rich production are: The *Fanitullsuite* for Violin (1946), a *Serenade* for Violin, Clarinet and Bassoon (1947), *Overture* for Orchestra (1950), *Ballet Music Suite* (1952), *Sonata no. 2 and 3 for Violin* (1956–1959), *Divertimento for Flute* (1958), and the *String Quartet* (1959). His *4th Violin Concerto* dates from 1961, and is dedicated to the memory of Carl Flesch. His great opera *Atlantis* should also be mentioned.

The two composers we are to deal with now represent an interesting and significant combination in several ways. They have been the leading personalities in Norwegian music since the last war, and they still occupy a central position. During and at the end of the war they were both aiming strongly at national

Harald Sæverud   Photo: Norsk Telegrambyrå

expression in their music, but whereas the elder of them, *Harald Sæverud,* started as an international-ist and then gradually became more and more convinced of the possibilities of a typically Norwegian music, the younger, *Klaus Egge,* has been moving in virtually the opposite direction in his music. But he still claimed that the idiom of his compositions is saturated by genuine native

Norwegian components. He said in a letter written in 1965: "My view of 'the national' is rather wide. For instance, I consider my Violin Concerto to be 'Norwegian'. The folklore elements are relatively abstract, but they *are* there. In this case we might use the term 'metamorphosis of Norwegian material', in the same sense that Bartók's later string quartets are a kind of metamorphosis of material that is basically Hungarian. If I had not examined the 'Norwegian' elements and analysed them before writing this Concerto, it would not have had the character it has now."

Harald Sæverud (born 1897) is today regarded by the general public as one of the most truly Norwegian of our modern composers. Yet he is far from being dependent on any pattern from our folk music. "When a man composes straight from his heart, and is a Norwegian, his music must be Norwegian too." "I have never had any desire to imitate the patterns of folk music, but I have tried to absorb its spirit, not its special features." These are quotations from his frequent utterances about the core of his art, the most definite being: "I do not use folk tunes, I create my own!"

Harald Sæverud underwent a long period of development before reaching this standpoint. He began composing in a rather common mid-European style. His first symphony, from 1920, of which only the second movement is performed nowadays, under the title *Ouvertura Appassionata,* was, like his 2nd *Symphony* (1923), characterized by the contemporary critics as "approaching the line from Mahler to Krenek". In the late 1920s he was especially preoccupied with the question of atonality, as is reflected in his opus 6, a piano suite, and the *Cello Concerto* opus 7. In these the polyphony is prominent. However, he felt that this medium did not suit him, and reverted to a style based on an extended tonality, still with strong polyphonic and highly dissonant elements. This is apparent in his *Fifty Small Variations,* opus 8. By 1940 his list of works has reached opus 13, among them the *Canto Ostinato* (1934) in which the voice of a European predominates, but where some modal phrases reminiscent of church music remind us to some extent of Norwegian folk music.

However, it was the years of the German occupation of Norway, 1940–45, which revolutionized Sæverud's attitude. The truly Norwegian element comes out most sharply during these years. Sæverud himself has said: "When the Germans invaded Norway, a real rage of productivity was immediately released in me. I felt that my work had to be a personal war with Germany." His patriotism found immediate expression in a large number of piano pieces collectively entitled 'Slåtter og Stev fra Siljustöl'. As an introduction to these the composer has written: "They are not folk melodies, but entirely my own productions, created at Siljustöl, my estate. They must not be considered as folklore, but rather strictly classical, a fact which is obvious from the extensive use of two-part counterpoint. However, the scenery of western Norway, so fraught with rugged temperament, makes the use of a sort of intensifying rubato necessary. The tunes must, so to speak, be allowed to run amok, even if they only do so in order to underline rhythm and character."

Together with these piano pieces appeared a series of 'airs' for orchestra: Siljuslåtten, opus 17, Galdreslåtten, opus 20, and last but not least Kjempeviseslåtten, dedicated to the men and women of the Resistance Movement. Originally it was part of the Piano Pieces opus 22, but has been transformed into an orchestral piece in its own right. In Sæverud's music we now find diatonic themes, a harmony that moves outside the usual logic of cadence and is strongly marked by dissonance, but far from atonal. We should perhaps call it a greatly extended tonality. In the presentation of melody we meet a technique of repetition which can remind us of primitive music. The melody often consists of a series of interrelated motifs, developed in a way that brings to mind the vek technique of Norwegian folk music. During the war he also wrote most of the symphonic trilogy consisting of the Symphony No. 5, Quasi una fantasia (1941) with the subtitle "Resistance Movement Symphony", and Symphony No. 6 (1942), composed in memory of his close friend Audun Lavik, who was shot by the Germans. This symphony is best known under its subtitle Sinfonia Dolorosa. His Symphony No. 7, "Salme" (Hymn), edited in 1947, has two subtitles: "Father's and Mother's Symphony" and "The Symphony of Privation and Struggle, Faith and Gratitude".

In this trilogy Sæverud shows that he has an entirely independent conception of symphonic form. It strikes us at once that he has adopted the single movement form instead of using several movements, and that he treats his material with the greatest possible concentration. "The single movement represents the whole symphony", he has declared. "The various main parts within the sonata form are expanded to a degree which makes them approach independent movements." Of definite significance is the use of the variation idea, particularly in the transition part.

The most sensational of Sæverud's works from the early postwar period is undoubtedly the music to Ibsen's *"Peer Gynt"*, music as Norwegian as Grieg's, though entirely different. It was written for a performance of Ibsen's play in 1946, aiming at a presentation stripped of all romanticism. Sæverud's result is more realistic and true to life, judged by modern ears. We need only compare his "Anitra's dance" with that of Grieg, which gives a very idealized and decorative picture of the girl, while Sæverud presents her through wild exotic rhythms. This gives a more apposite picture of the Bedouin girl who, as one critic said, "when all is said and done, almost certainly appeared rather ragged and rough, and had dirty feet". Solveig's song is also unaccompanied, as a diatonic melody, though not based on major or minor keys. In the music for Dovregubben's Hall he exploits the most unusual orchestral effects, and in "Mixed Company", which symbolizes Peer Gynt's journeying around the world, he has with wit and skill interwoven various national anthems into a lively international discussion. His "Peer Gynt" music has since been arranged in a Suite of 12 movements which has been acclaimed in concert halls far and wide.

Mention should also be made of his music for Ibsen's "Emperor and Galilean", his music for the film "Havretunet" and his ballet *Knight Bluebeard and his Nightmare*. Further works by Sæverud are the *Second Piano Concerto* (1950), the orchestral work *Poema Eroica* (1955), *the Violin Concerto* (1956) and his *8th Symphony* (1958), commissioned for the celebration of the Centenary of Minnesota, USA, hence usually called The Minnesota Symphony. His 9th *Symphony* was first presented at the Bergen Festival in

Klaus Egge
Photo: Norsk Telegrambyrå

1966, but after being thoroughly revised it had a new world premiere in 1968. Sæverud has also composed concertos for violincello, bassoon, and oboe. The most important other works to appear during the 1970s are three *String Quartets* and the *Mozart-Motto-Sinfonietta,* op. 58.

The development of the personal style of *Klaus Egge* (1906–1979) represents, as we mentioned earlier, almost the reverse of that of Harald Sæverud. What is common to both of them, and common as a general tendency in post-war music, is the pre-dominance of a contrapuntal pattern, a polyphonic manner of handling themes and motifs, and not least — particularly in recent years — a predilection for variation technique, frequently described by the composers concerned as 'metamorphosis'. The root of this may be found in the fact that Norwegian folk tunes were conceived and performed unaccompanied, with no consi-deration of harmonies.

Klaus Egge's starting point was, literally as well as metaphoric-ally, on solid Norwegian rock. Born and brought up in a district where national traditions in folklore — folk music and other aspects — were alive and carefully fostered, he was, as he said himself much later in life, to be mentally part of the milieu which was the source of his mother's milk.

He developed a style which does not follow the cadence system but which is motivated exclusively by the natural contrapuntal contrasts which create contrasts in music.

As a polyphonic composer he cultivates the principle of melody strongly combined with a rhythmic driving force. The melodic material is taken from or formed in accordance with Norwegian folk music and is developed through the characteristic forms of this music. The peculiarities of Norwegian folk tunes derive from small divergencies within certain typical intervals in the scale, and based on this and as an adaptation of characteristic traits in the "airs" for Hardanger fiddle, where the melodies are often composed of various four-note series or tetrachords, Egge has built scale-types of tetrachords with these features. However, he has, through the addition of various such tetrachords, constructed extended scales that — over two octaves — give all the 12 semi-tones. This means that even though the counterpoint is always diatonic, i.e. the contrapuntal structure of the music possesses the features of Norwegian folk music, the harmonies have full chromatic tension.

These features are already found in his "Draumkvede" sonata for piano (1934), and in a number of other works from the 1930s, including a piano concerto, opus 9, and a chamber symphony (both of them now rejected by the composer).

We find his "Norse" style even more convincing in the dramatic *Sveinung Vreim,* for soloists, choir and orchestra, op. 11, his *Tvo-røystes Slåtterytmer* (two-part folk dance phantasies) op. 12 for piano, and the powerful *Noregssongen,* op. 16, for male choir, written to the patriotic poem "Gud signe Noregs land" (God bless Norway). The choice of texts for the vocal compositions underlines his will to create *Norwegian* music, as do the folk dance models for his piano pieces. The most elaborate works of this kind are his *Phantasy in Halling,* in *Springar* and in *Gangar.* However, the characteristic traits mentioned for the music above are also significant for his chamber works of the pre-war period: the *Sonata for Violin and Piano* (1932) and the *Piano Trio* (1941). From the later period — after 1950 — dates a second piano sonata, *Sonata Patetica,* op. 27.

During the war, and since, Klaus Egge has decidedly turned to the major forms. First came his *Symphony No. 1,* opus 12, composed in 1941—42 and dedicated to "the Norwegian seamen who took part in the great World War". It is in memory of his childhood friend who lost his life at sea, and in an analysis of his work the composer uses expressions which give us not only a good picture of the meticulous construction of the work, but also of the very nature of the music and the feelings that have created it. Terms such as "thematic struggle", "top tension", "fighting one's way up", "whipped up" and so forth are constantly cropping up. A dynamic, volcanic, aggressive display of strength is the hallmark of Egge. His constructive intelligence is not of the bloodless kind, the driving force is a vigorous temperament and virile forcefulness. This is implicit even in his *Symphony No. 2,* called Sinfonia Giocosa, and *Symphony No. 3,* called the Louisville Symphony because it is a work commissioned for the Louisville Symphony orchestra. His *4th Symphony* is also a commissioned work, this time for Detroit.

The *Symphony No. 5* was commissioned by the Philharmonic Society of Oslo and had its world premiere at one of the concerts in connection with the celebration of the Society's 50th anniversary. This symphony differs to quite an extent from the previous ones, as the composer deliberately intended to show a new side. He named the symphony *Sinfonia dolce con passacaglia.*

One of the most frequently performed of Klaus Egge's works is his *Piano Concerto No. 2,* opus 21. It is in the form of symphonic variations and fugue on the theme of a Norwegian folk tune. The fugue is in unusually free form, and the piano does not participate actively in the fugal development; this is indicated in the title of this part of the work: Finale Concertante contra Fuga. Egge has also written a *Concerto for Violin* (1953) and a *Cello Concerto* (1966) commissioned by the Norwegian Broadcasting Corporation for the celebration of his sixtieth birthday.

There is also a third *Piano Concerto,* op. 32, from 1974, and from the same year a *Sonatina for Harp.* From 1976 dates his second *Wind Quintet.*

At this point it seems logical to mention some other composers who are idiomatically related to the group.

Sverre Jordan
Photo: Norsk Komponistforening

Harald Lie (1902–1942) died just before his 40th birthday, and this meant the loss of one of the most talented members of his generation. He had by then completed 12 opuses, but had himself destroyed the first two. His *Symphony* from 1936 showed a definite talent for handling this form, which he developed further in his *Symphony No. 2*, first performed in 1938. His *Symphonic Dance* for orchestra has been performed rather frequently, and his song for soprano and orchestra *Skinnvengbrev* (A Bat's Letter), today certainly the most frequently performed of his works, has been on the repertoires of all leading Norwegian sopranos since Kirsten Flagstad. In this work he displays his thouroughly symphonic way of thinking, as the whole dramatic and violent crescendo of song is developed from a single short motif.

Sverre Jordan (1889–1972) came onto the musical scene together with Fartein Valen, David Monrad Johansen, and Arne Eggen. Whereas Fartein Valen became and remained the great revolutionary in Norwegian music, forcing himself through and away from the bonds of tradition, Monrad Johansen was the decided opposite, not only by keeping to the traditions, but by working as his ideal for a more profound understanding of the essential value of this tendency in the art of a nation. Sverre Jordan represents a freer attitude between these two extremes; in his young days he was declared by some critics to be a radical, although in 1921 a more perceptive analyst, Gerhard Schjelderup (see p. 48) characterized Jordan as a moderate lyricist. He pointed out works by Jordan showing an essential aspect of the composer's art, namely his songs, more than 200 in number, some with piano, others with orchestral accompaniment. Several of them have gained lasting popularity and can be found on the concert repertoires of singers such as Kirsten Flagstad or Lauritz Melchior. But apart from songs and small instrumental pieces, Sverre Jordan has composed sonatas for piano, for violin and piano, flute and piano, 2 piano trios, 2 piano concertos, a good number of orchestral works, dramatic music, and two melodramas. Of his orchestral works the suite *Holberg Silhuetter* (Holberg Silhouettes), depicting characters from Holberg's comedies, is the most frequently performed.

Jordan treats the sonata form in the traditional way of composers belonging to the classicistic line of the Romantic period, often with traces of national peculiarities, even if these are less penetrating than within the declared national romantic group of our composers.

We still have to mention some of the composers born between the beginning of this century and the outbreak of World War I. Some of them are still active, and have already long ago found a personal style which they alter only to a very small extent, while others are open to new ideas arising from the general development of European music. Their most noticeable common characteristic is the fact that the special traits in their styles which may be said to have a definite *Norwegian* character are gradually becoming less significant, and there are few of them, if any, who still consider this as important in the evaluation of their music.

Karl Andersen (1903–1970) has — as was the case with Bjarne Brustad — obtained his thorough knowledge of symphonic music and orchestration problems in the course of many years of activity as solo cellist with the Oslo Philharmonic Orchestra. His first composition for orchestra dates back to 1922 *(Two Norwegian Dances),* but he himself maintains that his mature works began with the *String Quartet* (1935), continuing with the *Chamber Symphony* (1936), and the *Suite for Orchestra* (1937), a work which brought him the first prize in a competition arranged by the Norwegian Composers' Society and the Norwegian Broadcasting Corporation.

Later works of significance are the *Trio for Flute, Clarinet and Cello* from 1939, *Vårdagen* (The Spring Day), a song for male chorus, composed in 1942, and the *Festival Overture,* which in 1950 secured him a prize in a competition arranged in connection with the celebration of Oslo's 900th anniversary and the inauguration of the new City Hall.

Whilst Karl Andersen's first works have definite affinities with the national romantic trend, he gradually turns to a more modernistic style, beginning with his *Trio* of 1939, without giving up the nationalistic character completely. This happens only around 1960, after he had worked for a time with twelve-tone technique. His first work in this style dates from 1961, a piano piece called *Colombine and the Wicked Harlequin.* The same style is apparent in his 3rd *String Quartet* from 1966 and the *Variations on Theme and Rhythm.* This work is not orthodox twelve-tone music, but composed rather in a free atonal style.

Erling Kjellsby (1901–1976) may also be said to belong to this school. He has devoted himself mainly to chamber music, and of his four *String Quartets* nos. 2 and 3 are frequently performed. They represent 'absolute music', not only formally but also as regards the expressional side. They were composed during the Occupation of 1940–45, when most of the other composers were writing music reflecting the feelings of suppressed rage, despair and deep sorrow. However, Erling Kjellsby says about his quartets: "I have never written such bright and hopeful music. 'An escape from reality?' you might ask. No: a flight into reality, away from the nightmare world which the Occupation formed in the minds of Norwegians. I kept in mind the bright happy reality which we knew would come."

Besides chamber music Kjellsby has written a *Chaconne and Fugue* for orchestra, as well as a *Norwegian Rhapsody,* works for piano and organ, and songs for choir and for solo voices with piano accompaniment.

Conrad Baden (born 1908) is among the composers who have studied orchestration with Bjarne Brustad. As late as 1951–52 he studied composition in Paris with Honegger and Rivier. Up to this time Baden's compositions were mainly in the fields of chamber and church music: *Sonata for Violin and Piano,* a *Piano Trio* and two *String Quartets.* His most important church music consists of some organ works and his *Mass* from 1953, in which he introduces a more modern tone into the otherwise rather conservative style of church music in Norway.

After his sojourn in Paris Baden's interest in writing for orchestra was aroused, and this resulted in a series of orchestral compositions, containing a *Divertimento,* a *Concertino* for Clarinet and Strings, *Concerti* for Violin, Piano and Bassoon with orchestra, as well as a *Concerto per Orchestra,* a *Fantasia Breve per Orchestra,* and *Intrada Sinfonica.* Between 1953 and 1980 he wrote 6 symphonies; the latest will have its world premiere in 1982. His list of chamber music works is equally extensive and varied, both regarding structure and choice of instruments. As a church musician he has also enriched this field of Norwegian music with several works for organ, motets, a Mass and other types of shorter choral songs. In these works we may find some influence from Palestrina's style, well integrated in his personal style. In Baden's later works the polyphonic elements give way to a style based more on constructive combinations of sound, as is the case in his *Intrada Sinfonica.*

Even though they were born considerably later, there is reason to mention two more composers here, since in their attitude they have declared their support for the stylistic characteristics of the group we have been dealing with up to this point.

Edvard Fliflet Bræin (1924—1976) was the son of a composer and organist who gave him a solid training along classical lines, a great respect for traditions, and a warning to keep away from all sorts of suspect and dangerous avant-garde inventions. This probably restricted his highly gifted son to a moderate line which kept him unfairly in the shadow of those of his contemporaries who attract attention by means of more revolutionary music. Still, Bræin's works are always received with full acclamation by the public. Although his own life story was not altogether happy, a definite trait in his character was a good sense of humour, a capacity for bringing to the fore the lighter sides of human behaviour. This is evident in his opus one, a *Serenade*, "The Merry Musicians". Yet his attitude to composing music was serious enough. Among his many orchestral works we find four symphonies, — no. 1 dates back to 1950, no. 4 was composed in 1968. Throughout the symphonies he maintains inherited forms, though in a way which may be labelled Neo-classical.

Other instrumental works which must be mentioned are a *Concerto Overture*, a *Small Overture*, another *Serenade*, this time for orchestra, and a *Cappriccio for Piano and Orchestra*. An outstanding place in his later production is occupied by two operas, *Anne Pedersdotter*, based on a historical drama, and *Den Stundesløse* (The Busybody), based on a comedy by Ludvig Holberg. Together they give a convincing picture of the versatility of the mature artist. Whereas the first has an intensive, tragic, dramatic content, the second is full of wit and shows Fliflet Bræin's artistic capability to create humour in music. Both have been performed at the Norwegian State Opera.

Besides the influence of his father and his beloved teacher in Oslo, Bjarne Brustad, Fliflet Bræin points out what Shostakovich taught him about the value of simplicity, and David Monrad Johansen (as well as his father) of the importance of folk music elements in art music.

Tor Brevik (born 1932) considered in his younger years that Carl Nielsen had a particular influence on his development through his unique handling of intervals. At the same time he felt indebted to Bartók, Hindemith and to some extent Stravinsky. In view of such statements it is natural to find Tor Brevik among the definitely moderate modernists, putting the stress on linear movement. With his fine melodic vein this will be not only natural, but for him *the* trend to follow. Apart from one of his compositions, the *Elegy* for soprano and chamber orchestra (from 1965) he has shown little interest in instrumental effects and sound experiments. Up to 1970 the works that stand most central on his list are for orchestra, beginning with the *Overture* from 1950, later followed by a *Serenade* (1959), and a *Concertino* for Clarinet and String Orchestra (1961). There is also a *Concertino* for strings, from 1967, as well as an *Intrada* from 1969.

During the 1970s Brevik composed a good deal of music for the stage and television. There is ballet music, a children's opera and a TV film, from the music for which also came an orchestral suite, the *Senja-Suite*. Finally mention should be made of a prologue, *Man and Music,* for choir and orchestra, from 1978, and Brevik's early chamber music.

Finn Arnestad (born 1915) considers himself almost self-taught, although he went through solid studies in organ, piano, and violin as well as in composition at the Music Conservatory of Oslo. Still he divides his years of education and evolution into two main stages, the receptive, when he had teachers, and the productive, when his method was to put into practice musical ideas, evaluating them from the point of view of quality, thus augmenting his experience. Besides, he has studied profoundly the works of J. S. Bach, Mozart and Beethoven; later he was strongly affected by the music of Debussy and Stravinsky. He has also been influenced to a very great extent by Fartein Valen and Anton Webern.

This solid and searching development predicts the kind of music his mature period as a composer has brought. He tries new ideas, takes them up in order to evaluate them, but never takes them up just because they are new. On principle he wants to maintain continuity with the past. Thus he considers conventional notation as the most adequate means of expression, even if it sometimes can seem complicated for a certain purpose. In his melodic lines he tries to avoid the stereotyped effect of a definite scale by combining diatonic, pentatonic and chromatic forms. He is also loyal to the demand of the twelve-tone technique not to repeat a note, but *if* he breaks this rule, it is in order to sharpen the impression of recognition. His system of harmony is based on what in the theory of sound waves is known by the term interferences, on what the physicists call 'onephased sound waves'.

Finn Arnestad himself does not want to point to any of his works as being more important than others. "The most important thing has always been, and will probably always be, the work I am occupied with at the moment."

Johan Kvandal (born 1919) has studied with Per Steenberg in Oslo, Joseph Marx in Vienna, and Nadia Boulanger in Paris. He works as an organist in Oslo and is a music critic for one of the daily newspapers.

In his first compositions he followed the Norwegian line of the 1930s, as we will realize when examining his first songs, piano pieces and also orchestral works like his *Norwegian Overture.* As David Monrad Johansen's son (see p. 57) he evidently received strong impressions from him and the circle around him in his young days. Kvandal himself stresses the important influence he feels he has received from Mozart and Stravinsky. "Besides their spiritual force, the clarity and the utter precision in which they express themselves have spellbound me above all", he once declared. After his studies with Nadia Boulanger he came to adopt a freer view of tonality. As from the beginning of the 1960s his style leaves the national tendencies in order to obtain richer means of expression through the much freer use of tonality parallel with sharper dissonant harmonies.

However, with the music for the dramatization of Alexander Kielland's "Skipper Worse" (commissioned by Norwegian television) as well as the *Tre Slåttefantasier* (Three Fantasies on Norwegian Dances) he returned apparently to domestic soil, yet with definitely richer experience. His work *Antagonia* for two string orchestras and percussion, op. 38, is an example of a synthesis of freer tonality and folklore elements. This came to be characteristic of his further development, as we realize in his *Violin Concerto,* op. 52.

Kvandal has been and continues to be a prolific composer, with works in many fields of music, apart from opera. Among his orchestral works, other than those already mentioned, are a *Symphony,* a *Symphonic Epos,* a *Concerto for Oboe,* and one for Flute and String Orchestra, an *Ibsen-cantata,* commissioned by the city of Skien, Ibsen's birthplace, on the occasion of the jubilee in 1978. There is music for piano; there are also two *String Quartets,* a String Quartet plus the national string instrument, the Hardingfele (see p.12), a *Quintet* for *Wind Instruments,* a *Flute Quartet,* and *Night Music* for 8 wind instruments plus double bass.

Hallvard Johnsen (born 1916) has the flute as his main instrument, and has appeared as soloist on this instrument on many occasions. During the years when he studied the flute he also had lessons in music theory. His opus one, *Suite* for Flute, Violin and Viola, was performed at his debut recital in Oslo in 1941. Between 1938, when he composed this trio, and 1956, he composed in the more conservative nationalistic style, but he gradually felt that this had definite limits. It led him to compose in some sort of routine, and finally meant stagnation. In search of wider orientation he became interested in dodecaphony, and after labouring with this he felt he could develop a personal way of expression by using this freely, not binding himself to the serial technique. He feels a certain demand for a tonal centre, and thus he may actually be said to compose rather in a free tonal style, however extended the tonality may be.

For the final forming of his style, studies with the Danish composer Vagn Holmboe were undoubtedly of decisive importance. He keeps to the accepted classical forms, preferring the sonata form combined with the kind of variation technique which among his contemporaries is labelled "Metamorphosis". Up to the year 1981 he has composed 89 works. Most of these are in larger forms, such as 12 *Symphonies, Concertos,* two for Violin, two for Flute, one for Violoncello and one for trumpet and Orchestra. In the field of chamber music there are three *String Quartets* and a *Quintet for Wind Instruments and Vibraphone.* Johnsen has written two operas, of which the second dates from 1981 and is numbered op. 89. The first one, for which Hallvard Johnsen has also written the libretto, based on a novel by Alfred Hauge, the composer prefers to call an oratorio-opera. He has also written two other oratorios, *Krosspåske* for baritone solo, choir and orchestra, and *Logos,* for soli, mixed choir, organ and orchestra. Johnsen has also composed a melodrama, based on Ibsen's "Bergmannen", for one male voice and orchestra.

Knut Nystedt (born 1915) studied composition first in Norway, then in 1947 he went to the USA to study with Aaron Copland. Besides composition he has undertaken extensive studies in organ playing and has for years been active both as a church organist and as a performing concert artist on this instrument. In 1950 he founded the chamber choir *Det norske solistkor* and has

Knut Nystedt
Photo: Norsk Komponistforening

since been its artistic leader and conductor and has brought it up
to a standard which has secured it solid successes on many tours
in Europe and the USA. Since 1964 he has been teaching choral
conducting at the Faculty of Music of Oslo University.

Nystedt is, from inner conviction as well as through his daily
work, strongly bound to church music. His major compositions
for choir and vocal soloists are mainly based on texts from the
Bible or connected with sacred subjects: his op. 36, *Brennofferet*
(Burnt Offering), is a biblical tableau for recitation, choir and
orchestra. His op. 46, *De Syv Segl* (The Seven Seals), is a vision
for orchestra, and its world premiere took place in the USA in
1962. Of his many choral works at least 50 per cent have been
published in the USA, where he has won a great reputation not
least among the university choirs. From the 1970s date *Et Samisk
Dies Irae* for 4 choirs, wind instruments and percussion, and a
Norwegian *Te Deum* for choir and orchestra, as well as two
Masses. Considering his position as an outstanding concert organist, it is relevant to find a list of important compositions for this
instrument, or the use of it in several combinations. We also find
some fine examples of chamber music, among them 4 *String
Quartets.* A work that attracts special attention is *Pia Memoria,* a
requiem for 9 brass instruments.

Other works which should be mentioned are op. 52, *The Moment,* for soprano, celesta and percussion, his op. 54, *De Profundis* for mixed choir, and op. 58, *Lucis Creator Optime*, for soloists, choir and orchestra, composed for the celebration of the centenary of Augsburg College in Minneapolis in 1969.

Since his first mature compositions Knut Nystedt has gone through quite a remarkable stylistic development. His *Høgfjell-Suite* (The High Mountains) from 1940–41 is moderately nationalistic, whereas works appearing since World War II turn to neoclassical idioms. His *Concerto Grosso* for 3 trumpets and string orchestra, from 1946, and the *Symphony for Strings* from 1949 are examples. Characteristic of all his works is his strong expressive will, which appears most clearly in his symphonic picture *Spenningens Land* (The Land of Tension) from 1947. However, since the middle of the 1950s Nystedt has evidently been examining his status and been searching for new, richer or at least different means of expression. In *Brennofferet* he uses pentatonic steps, and as from *De Syv Segl,* that is to say from 1958—60, he leaves tonality and develops his material on dodecaphonic series. There is no doubt that the sound colours fascinate him particularly, as will be heard from his orchestral work *Collocations,* and the choral work *De Profundis* from 1964, a work for a cappella choir where he uses cluster effects around a simple Gregorian melody.

There were good reasons for beginning this chapter by discussing a composer who belongs chronologically to an earlier group. There are equally good reasons for beginning the following section of the chapter with a composer who, considered from the point of view of both age and style, belongs to an older generation than those we have been dealing with.

Pauline Hall (1890—1969) is in some ways unique. In a period when the German influence was as predominant as it had been ever since Kjerulf's and Grieg's pilgrimages to Leipzig, she turned to France, and returned a devoted admirer of and believer in the current tendencies in French music. This is clearly reflected in her early works, such as the *Verlaine Suite* (1929) where we meet the brightly coloured world of Impressionism. This work vividly brings to life the soft euphony of Verlaine's poetry. Most

Pauline Hall
Photo: Norsk Telegrambyrå

noticeable is the wealth of delicate details in the orchestration, a trait also to be found in the cheerful informal suite *Circus Pictures* (1933).

Partly through her music, and partly as one of the country's leading critics, she came to represent a definite revolt against traditions in Norwegian music, not least by showing a demonstrative lack of understanding for the severe nationalism prevailing in the period 1920—30 (in many cases even longer, as we have seen). Her motto was a definite 'Look to Europe'. As correspondent for daily newspapers she lived in Berlin from 1926 to 1932, and the extremely rich musical and theatrical life there certainly widened her horizon even more.

The most far-reaching practical result of her experiences and of the conviction she had gained was the initiative she took in 1938 in getting a Norwegian section of the ISCM (International Society for Contemporary Music) started. She was the president of this section (in Norway called "Ny Musikk") until 1959, and her indefatigable work through these 21 years can hardly be estimated highly enough. Where the ordinary concert audiences were lacking, she created a slowly increasing circle of music-lovers

89

who understood the importance of supporting the young creative artist going new ways, and gradually they even felt they
understood the music she created. Besides this activity on the
inner front, she was also extremely able at winning remarkable
victories on the harder outer front where she had to fight against
public opinion and all sorts of official sluggishness and lack of
interest and understanding.

All her work in this respect may have hampered her creative
force. After 1930 she was first of all active as a composer of
theatre music. Here she displays her profound knowledge of the
capabilities of individual instruments. She is undoubtedly one of
the most important and prolific composers of modern music for
the theatre in Norway. With extreme skill, she knows how to
combine a few instruments in an exquisite way, giving just the
sound effects the scene in question wants. She has written music
for a long list of dramas, from classical Greek via several of
Shakespeare's plays to modern literature, including of course
several Norwegian plays, and also films, but in only few cases this
music has found its way to the concert hall. This is certainly due
partly to the special instrumentation, varying from piece to piece,
partly to the unbreakable connection between play and music.
There is one exception, a work which is among her chefs d'oeuv-
re of orchestral music: the *Julius Cæsar* suite, written for full
orchestra for concert performances.

Pauline Hall's affinity for literature has naturally resulted in a
good number of songs, both for solo voice and for choir. Her
well-developed sense of humour comes through in some songs
for male choir as well as in her setting of a collection of *Tosserier*
(nonsense poetry) by Halfdan Rasmussen. For chamber music
groups she has composed a *Suite for 5 Wind Instruments* (1945)
and later a *Small Dance Suite* for oboe, clarinet and bassoon.

The composers to follow (in the footsteps of Pauline Hall, so to
speak) are those who are most decidedly concerned with the idea
of creating a New Music, in the spirit of Pauline Hall, as a
representative of the ideals of the ISCM: to move forwards, to be
free from ties of tradition and rules that are not perpetual. They
do it each in their own way, to some extent, even if they may

follow more general tendencies in western music. It therefore seems natural to mention them in chronological order, even if some of the older composers actually came on the musical scene rather late.

Bjørn Fongaard (1919—1980) had the guitar as his special instrument, and was a frequent performer. He also held a diploma, obtained in 1947, from the conductors' class at the Music Conservatory of Oslo. Ever since 1941 he was active both as a performing artist and as a student of music theory. In composition he started in the style of Palestrina, and subsequently went through all the most important changing styles up to our time, when Bjarne Brustad opened his mind to the loosening of strict tonality by using bi- and polytonal constructions. From then on his further development is out of the ordinary. What led him to this was partly studies of Hindemith's theories, partly studies with Karl Andersen in 12-tone composing. In this period Fongaard composed several works for chamber ensembles, and *Vision* for cello and piano, performed in 1961.

However, Fongaard steadily penetrated into the utmost possibilities inherent in the tone material, through neat analyses and mathematical evaluation, hence utilizing his theoretical achievements as a creative artist. Scientifically minded, he constructed a quartertone guitar and used it both in his *Inventions* for guitar and the symphonic poem *Uran* 235. In this work the use of quartertone material is consciously based on the harmonic overtone-row and its natural intervals, both in sound combinations and functionally.

He seems to have reached his final goal in 1965—66, when subdividing the octave into an infinite number of intervals. In what he named his "n-tonal system" the intervals can be reduced to any desired degree. Again he constructed a guitar, his so-called micro-guitar, which thanks to its sound and technical qualities produces tone material which is nearly identical with the sound sources of electronic and concrete music. The only difference will be that music performed on a micro-guitar is produced in the traditional way, not in a laboratory, and the composer considers this immediate contact with the musical material very important.

Having reached his complete freedom of expression, the composer produced in quick succession a series of works based on his "n-tonal system": *Galaxy, Homo Sapiens, Epos, Opus Microtonale, Aphorisms, Reflexions* for recitation and micro-guitar, and the TV ballet *Relief*. The composer considered *Kosmos,* for orchestra, particularly important. He had this to say: "The complete freedom of intervals which is present both in linear and harmonic structures permits a tonal development where cadence functions exist in a highly differentiated way." Of *Reflexions*, composed in 1967, he declared: "I consider this work of special importance since the music is programmatically coordinated with a profound searching for truth: musical feeling and rational thinking are combined in the music as one mental activity. At times this has been looked upon as incompatible, but our time is realizing more and more that this phenomenon is a natural expression of the indivisibility of art, science and technology in our society."

Of his latest works may be mentioned a ballet from 1972, *Dimensions,* and several *Concertos* where he combines tape recording, pre-recorded on a micro-guitar, with the solo instruments. On his impressive list of works, considered both from the high opus numbers and the strong personality reflected in them, we also find combinations for "normal" instruments.

Edvard Hagerup Bull (born 1922) has for most part of his mature years been living and studying outside Norway, partly in Germany, partly in France. He left the Conservatoire National Supérieur de Musique in Paris in 1952 with the Prix de Composition from the class of Darius Milhaud, who together with Jean Rivier has meant much for his career in the musical life of France, with which he has — and has shown — great affinity. He has had several French state scholarships, as well as some from Germany, giving him the chance to study for two years at the Musikhochschule in Berlin under Boris Blacher. A great honour was bestowed upon him when in 1968 the French government commissioned a work from him. Such a "commande d'Etat" is only very rarely given to a non-French composer. For Hagerup Bull several more have followed, as well as from other official institutions, including some from other countries.

Even if Hagerup Bull is full of gratitude towards the masters he has been in touch with, as well as some other composers of his own generation, he wants to be, and feels, completely free. Today he considers himself an independent composer, completely uninfluenced by specific traditions and modes of expression. Still he has a keen appreciation of all currents and trends of the 20th century. Complex nuances, rhythms and dynamism characterize his music. This liberty is, according to Hagerup Bull, the only possibility for developing genuine ideas, and for him the idea, its content, is always the source on which the technical development should be based. Not least in his works from the 1960s and 1970s is his personal engagement in what happens in the world reflected, and this often thoroughly permeates the musical expression.

This is the case with works like *Epilogue*, for strings, *A la Mémoire d'un Monde Perdu, also Sinfonia Humana*, which the composer himself considers as one of his most fundamental works. Also his personal affection and admiration for colleagues has served as inspiration for some major works, like *Chant d'hommage à Jean Rivier* and *In Memoriam Edvard Fliflet Brœin*. The latest work of this kind, up to now, dates from 1981, *Lamentazione*, with the subtitle "Pour la Pologne et la Solidarité".

From Hagerup Bull's extensive list of works should be mentioned his six *Symphonies*, of which Lamentazione, for strings, is no. 6. Further there are two *Ballets* based on some of H. C. Andersen's fairy tales, several *Concertos* and some *Chamber Music*. Although his creative force leads to a steadily and fast growing series of new works, we should not forget some of the earlier opuses, like the suites *The Tin Soldier, Escapades, Sinfonia De Teatro* from 1951 and *Trois Mouvements Symphoniques* from 1955.

Antonio Bibalo was born in Trieste in 1922. He is now a Norwegian citizen, having settled in Norway more than 15 years ago. He studied composition and the piano, first at the conservatory in Trieste and then under Elizabeth Lutyens in London. In the Wieniawski Composers' Competition in Warsaw in 1954 he won a prize for his *Fantasy* for violin and orchestra, and the year after another prize, this time for his *Violin Concerto* in one movement, in the Béla Bartók Composers' Competition at Bloomington, USA.

In his young days Bibalo was particularly attracted by composers such as Bartók, Stravinsky and Debussy. Today he has no special individual preference, but admires what is new, be it composers or ideas. His own style is very free and he avoids any form of dogmatism, even though he is very conscious of the value of the experience of composers both past and present. His music is not dominated by folklore elements: at the most one may trace some signs of his Slavonic descent. In his music he combines harmonic and melodic lines, based on free tonality, polytonality and twelve-tone technique, but all expressed with the technical construction and orchestration of today.

The works which have made him internationally known are first of all his works for the stage, the opera *The Smile at the Foot of the Ladder* and the ballet *Pinocchio,* based on a short story by Henry Miller. This ballet had its world premiere in February 1969 at the Hamburg Staatsoper. In the same year he completed the *Sinfonia Notturna,* commissioned by the city of Trieste for its fiftieth anniversary as an Italian city. From 1969 we also have his *Overture,* commissioned by the Norwegian Broadcasting Corporation as its contribution to an international series of works intended for performance by light orchestras but written by composers of serious music. The title of the overture indicates its dualism: borrowed from Goldoni's famous play, it is *The Servant of Two Masters.* In 1969 the National Concert Organisation commissioned a work for flute, piano, double-bass and vibraphone, *Autumnale.* Other important works by Bibalo are the *Concerto Allegorico* for violin and orchestra (in memory of Fartein Valen) and the *Elegy for a Space Age,* and yet another remarkable work is his *Pitture Astratte* for large orchestra, based on four contemporary paintings (by Hartung, Melloni, Sugay and Inger Sitter). His aim has been not to illustrate the paintings in the form of programme music, but to give expression to the inner feelings which are aroused when one looks at them.

Important works which have appeared since 1970 are his two operatic works *Miss Julie,* built on Strindberg's drama, and *Gjengangere* (on Henrik Ibsen's "Ghosts"). For the Norwegian Broadcasting Corporation he composed, in collaboration with Hartvig Kiran, a radio opera *Askeladden* (a kind of male Cinderella).

Egil Hovland and Finn Mortensen (right)
Photo: Norsk Telegrambyrå

In his composition Bibalo employs twelve-tone technique in a special way, without any trace of dogmatism, using the orchestral elements to create a pointillistic and resolved pattern of orchestration. Whereas the orchestration in some of his works may be solid, it is similar to that of chamber music when he comes to his operas, the first of which he wrote shortly after the violin concerto in the years 1958—62.

Finn Mortensen, who was also born in 1922, studied with Klaus Egge during World War II, and with Niels Viggo Bentzon in Denmark after the war. In his collection of compositions from the first half of the 1950s, most of which were performed for the first time at a concert in 1954, he makes it clear that his point of departure is in the extended polyphony of Hindemith.

Mortensen had already taken up dodecaphonic techniques during the late 1940s, but his break through and away from tonality involved an intense struggle with his material. The collection of works first performed in 1954 still has many traits which echo composers like Irgens Jensen and Klaus Egge: diatonic melodies, classicistic handling of thematic material, for instance, and his polyphonic as well as motivic development. The works in question are his *String Trio* from 1950, the *Wind Quintet* from 1951, and the *Sonata for Solo Flute* from 1953. His *Symphony, opus 5*, also belongs to this category, although it was not finished until 1957. Finn Mortensen has said that the composers who have meant most to his development are Bach, Bruckner, Schoenberg, Webern and Stockhausen, and if one bears this in mind one can understand that a composer with the conscientious sincerity of Mortensen, with his definite wish to be true to himself in his expression, needed some years to reach the stage attained by Stockhausen.

However, from 1956 he seems to feel really at home in dodecaphony, both as regards serial and aleatoric techniques, and in the period to follow he characterized his mode of expression as "New-serialism". In some commentaries to his *Suite for Wind Quintet,* from 1974, he talks of his "pointillist music". His productivity increases remarkably as from the *Piano Sonata* (1956) and the *Fantasy and Fugue* from 1958 — performed at the ISCM festival in 1960. The scope widens steadily during the 1960s: in *Evolution* from 1961 he works less with melodic lines and more with sonorities. His strong expressive will causes real sound eruptions in this and other works of the same kind. He puts stillness against violent explosions of sound. This is due to his description of serial music: "Serial music is athematic and non-cyclical music, organized to series which are deduced from the principle of the *reconciliation of extremes* (emphasis by author).

This came to practical realization in a series of chamber music works, *New-serialism I, II,* and *III,* as well as in works like his *Hedda*-kavalkade for large orchestra, from 1974–75, and the *Suite for Wind Quintet,* already mentioned, from 1974.

When the State Academy of Music was founded in 1973, Finn Mortensen came to hold the chair of professor of composition.

Egil Hovland (born 1924) is by no means an avant-gardist, but with his alert spirit and receptive mind he has taken up the ideas and followed the trends as they appear in the general development of European music, has examined them, assimilated what he has found valuable, and adapted and combined it in his own way. The milestones in his personal development are, according to his own statement, marked with the names Carl Nielsen, Bartók and Dallapiccola. He studied with Dallapiccola in 1959, his previous teachers being Bjarne Brustad, Vagn Holmboe in Denmark and Aaron Compland in the USA. If we combine his admiration for Carl Nielsen and Bartók with what is typical of his teachers before Dallapiccola we have at once a key to his stylistic characteristics up to the most definite turning point in his development, namely when he met Dallapiccola. Confusing the picture to some extent is the fact that with great technical skill he combines different styles or stylistic elements in one work, not least in his church music. We often find that Norwegian composers are organists who have their daily work in connection with the church, for which they naturally also compose to some extent. As far as Hovland is concerned, this is the case not only to some extent, but far beyond that. He has been immensely and incessantly active both at his organ desk, on the rostrum and not least at the writing desk. When he reached the age of 50, a book was edited as part of the celebration, and there we find a complete list of works up to the year 1974. It fills 19½ pages: There is an ample variety of Masses, Cantatas, liturgical plays, Church opera and Ballet to be performed in a church, Hymns and other forms of liturgical music like Motets, of which there are 70, covering the whole liturgical year. What is also remarkable is his ability to adapt the structure of the works according to the foreseen use of the music, and this not only on account of the performers but also the listeners. Vox populi, participation by the community, is integrated. Some works are planned to be performed by children. Most of these works are commissioned for some special occasions, but have nevertheless shown qualities which have assured them of a continued existence in their own right.

If we just follow his development in "free" compositions, mainly instrumental, we ascertain his starting point as an expressive neoclassisist in his *Concerto for 3 Trumpets and Strings,* first performed at the ISCM festival in Strasbourg in 1958, two *Symphonies,* the *Suite for Flute and Piano,* and *Music for Ten Instruments.* We notice a gradual change from extended tonality or modality towards twelve-tone series, after · 1959 used both in defined serial technique and in the aleatoric manner. The colour in his music grows steadily richer, as does his emotional expression. His most important instrumental works to appear since 1959 are *Lamenti,* for orchestra, the *Wind Quintet, Variations for Two Pianos,* and *Elementa Pro Organo.*

In some works he deliberately combines stylistic elements, without working on the collage principle. Such a work is his *Vigilate* for choir, baritone and soprano solo, two dancers, organ and tape recording, composed for performance in a church. In this work Gregorian chant, tonal and dodecaphonic parts are placed side by side. Another work of this kind, *Rorate,* is for concertant organ, chamber orchestra with 4 percussions, 5 sopranos and electronic tape recording. For the 50th anniversary of the Philharmonic Society in Oslo, in September 1969, he composed his 3rd *Symphony,* for orchestra, choir and recitation, in one movment, based on a poem by Odd Medbøe and parts of the Book of Job. He has also written a suite, *Hiob* (Job) for recitation and organ, and as a result of his personal engagement it has been natural for him to seek sources of expression in religious texts. *Lilja,* words about love, from the Song of Songs, should be mentioned here: it was composed for recitation and orchestra, and commissioned by the Norwegian Broadcasting Corporation. The majority of his works, in fact, have come about either as commissions or as works written for special artists or ensembles.

Sigurd Berge (born 1929) studied composition with Finn Mortensen from 1956 to 1959; in 1965 he continued his studies in Copenhagen and Stockholm, and later at the University of Utrecht and in Poland, concentrating in the two last named places on electronic music and composition by means of computers. An immediate result of this is the use of electrophony in some of his works, and during the years 1968–71 he composed 21 short works which are exclusively electronic.

Through the years he has shown a definite interest in the

pedagogical side of musical activity, from a practical as well as a theoretical point of view. Among his earlier compositions we find *Chroma*, for symphony orchestra, of which one of the critics wrote after the first performance: "Through this work we have got a Norwegian parallel to The Young Person's Guide to the Orchestra, full of grotesque humour and rich fantasy. Along the same lines is *Epsilon*, composed for the school orchestra of the Rudolf Steiner School, and *Juvenus* for an amateur string orchestra, as well as some compositions for school brass bands. His interest in bringing children and young people in contact with present days' music during their school years has led to several books on Sound Creation for Teachers.

Returning to general list of works, his first work for symphony orchestra, *Pezzo Orchestrale,* is from 1958, *Raga,* for oboe and orchestra, was composed the year after, based on a study of Indian music. In 1961 appeared *Sinus,* for strings and percussion, and in 1963 *Chroma*. Some of his later works have not been performed in public because the musicians declared them "unplayable". The reason is that some of the effects he uses (knocking the body of the violins, as well as humming by the Members of the orchestra) did not appeal to the orchestra. Of his later works *Music for Orchestra* from 1978 was performed in 1981.

Of his chamber music *Yang Guan* aroused interest as an attempt to create expressions of pain, joy, friendship and leavetaking on the basis of a theme from a book on oriental music, a Chinese pentatonic melody. It is composed for wind quintet, and in 1969, three years after Yang Guan, he composed another wind quintet, this time for young people. And there we are back to what has already been mentioned earlier. He has composed ballet music for dancers and children, and a work entitled *Illuxit* is for children's choir, jazz piano and alp horn. In this connection we should mention his probably most frequently performed work *Hornlokk* (Horn Call) from 1972, an example of his solid affinity to the music of his native country. In 1981 a work from his birthplace in Norway was created and performed: *Gudbrandsdalsspelet* (The play from the valley of Gudbrandsdalen). 40 % of it is folk music, arranged and orchestrated, and 60 % is original composition, though based on popular tradition.

Arne Nordheim   Photo: Aftenposten

Arne Nordheim (born 1931) was educated at the Music Conservatory in Oslo, where his teachers in composition were Karl Andersen, Bjarne Brustad and Conrad Baden. Some visits to the Danish composer Vagn Holmboe have also been important for his development, which has been extraordinarily quick. A string quartet in 1956 and *Aftonland* (Evening Land) for soprano and chamber ensemble to a poem by Pär Lagerkvist from 1957 called public attention to his name. *Aftonland,* where sonoric combinations predominate, is particularly significant for his further development. This is evident in the first of his works to make its way outside the Nordic countries, his *Canzona for Orchestra,* composed in 1960. It was awarded the Bergen Festival prize for that year, and was performed at the ISCM Festival in 1963. According to the composer, he has been inspired by the Venetian Renaissance composer Giovanni Gabrieli: in particular by his use of concertante sound groups within an ensemble, the musical development being based on the principle of variation. This work established Nordheim as one of the most advanced orchestral expressionists, regarding both style and technique.

The prime reaction from the music public to his early works was to characterise him as an avant-gardist and his music as drastic and radical (and sometimes, indeed, to ask whether it was music at all). Nordheim himself has declared: "In *Canzona* as well as *Epitaffio* or *Katharsis,* with their electrophony, I built on experiences from what was Europe when I started composing, – and from the Europe of bygone days. Actually mere extrinsic idioms caused the idea of radical or drastic, the use of new means of expression, like the electrophony." Among Norwegian composers, at least up to his generation, he is the one who has most intensively and profoundly worked with this. At the age of 50 he declared that works like *Floating* or *Greening* (both from the 1970s) were the result of another way of reflecting on sound, different from what was the case before he worked with electrophony. It means, according to himself, greater ability to create sounds through more simple means. It is a matter of cutting out what earlier caused in-transparency.

A series of very varied and fascinating works appeared throughout the 1960s. He shows more and more clearly his wide perspectives, and his most vital imagination, where the aim of creating sound and movement seems to pervade. "Everything must sing" is one of the composer's favourite expressions. He wants to create works where sound, movement, light, and colours all play an important part. The central point of interest for the composer is to create spheres of sound corresponding to each other in certain ways, as well as musical movements matching each other in a refined pattern. He is extremely open to every kind of new technical equipment which gives possibilities for development. He undertakes himself some sort of basic artistic inquiries, but his goal will always be to find the most expressive means possible within the technical apparatus. "I look upon technical implements with the greatest romantic enthusiasm", says the composer.

In 1962 Nordheim wrote the ballet *Katharsis,* commissioned by the Norwegian State Opera, which performed it the same year, first at the Bergen Festival, then in Oslo in the autumn. Later the composer produced a suite for concert performance of the music. In this work Nordheim combines for the first time electrophonic sounds with orchestral ones, something which we will meet in several of his later works. An example is his *Epitaffio* from 1963, a work which has been performed in many countries both in and outside Europe, since its first performances in Stockholm in 1964 and at the ISCM Festival in Madrid the year after.

This work has as a motto a short verse by the Italian poet Quasimodo: "Each of us stands alone on the heart of Earth, pierced by a sunray, and suddenly it is evening." The three words Alone — Earth — Evening are his sonorific and emotional signals. Using the symphony orchestra combined with tape recordings he creates the wandering of light sound-groups towards darkness, clusters being linked to clusters underneath each other in slow modulations until at the end a quiet sound fills the whole room. The first part of the music is a great long crescendo leading up to an immense climax, then the further expiration descend towards stillness.

From what has been said previously about the composer's particular direction of interest and creative imagination, it is natural that he should turn to the type of works which combine music and the other arts. In 1965 he wrote *Favola,* a musical fable for 2 voices, 10 dancers, orchestra, electrophony and choir, commissioned by the Norwegian Television.

He returned to this type of work on several occasions, both before he composed music to *Katharsis,* and in his later production, partly using material from other orchestral works, as is the case in the two ballets he created in collaboration with the American choreographer Glen Tetley *(Strender* and *Greening).* The latest result of their collaboration to date is *The Tempest,* built (very freely) on Shakespeare's play, a work which fills a whole evening's performance. It had its world premiere during the Schwetzingen Festival in 1979, and a year later it was presented by the Norwegian State Opera, both in Oslo, Bergen and later in Copenhagen. Presentation in the USA is also planned.

Commissioned by the Netherlands' Dance Theatre, he wrote *Ariadne* in 1977. For stage performances of dramatic works he has composed music on a number of occasions, starting with Bjørnson's "Sigurd Slembe" and Molière's "Don Juan" in 1960. Of Ibsen's plays he has created music for "The Lady from the Sea", "Brand" and "Peer Gynt". For radio and TV theatre there is a long list of productions. The pause signal of the Norwegian Radio is also signed Arne Nordheim.

On the basis of electronic material which he created in the Utrecht studios in 1966 he composed his *Response I & II* in 1966 and 1968. Here he evaluates the sound contrasts and the ability to create a kind of instrumental dialogue in the concert hall. The first version is for two percussion groups and tape, two sound sources reacting on each other's activity, and in the course of the performance picking up ideas and repartees from each other, varying and transforming them. Sound modulations, extracted from the instruments of the two percussion groups, are fixed on the tape. By synchronizing the performance the effect should be that the sound emanating from the loudspeakers catches in a way the material delivered *in natura* by the percussion groups. He wants the work performed in a big hall, with a long time-delayed sound, even — if possible — in a group of rooms where the audience can move around and be surrounded by the sound as it is carried around the building by means of a control panel with several channels, controlling loudspeakers with powerful amplifiers all over the place. In *Response II* he has added an organ to the first version; a third version is for one percussion group + tape, whereas in the fourth version there are 4 percussionists. In the ballet *Strender* Nordheim uses some of the Response I music.

Throughout his mature years Arne Nordheim has been a most prolific composer. From his extensive list of works only some can be mentioned here. *Colorazione,* from 1967/68, is another work where electrophonic elements are combined with instruments (organ and percussion) and this is the case, too, with *Eco*, a work which the Swedish Broadcasting Corporation commissioned for the Stockholm Festival and the Nordic Music Festival in 1968. It is for mixed choir, children's choir, soprano solo and orchestra, to poems by Quasimodo. The following year the work was performed at the ISCM Festival in Hamburg. This performance and one at the Rostrum of Composers in Paris the same year enhanced his ever increasing international fame, making commissions more and more frequent.

Within this category appear works such as *Signals,* for accordion, percussion and electric guitar, commissioned by Rikskonserter, Stockholm (1968). The same year *Solitaire,* electronic music — A Play with Sound and Light — appeared as a commission in connection with the Sonja Henie-Onstad Art Centre, Oslo. 1970 was particularly rich in commissions: *Pace,* again an electronic work, was commissioned by the Polish Radio, *Floating,* a pure orchestral work, by the Danish Radio, and *Poly-Poly,* a very special electronic production for the Scandinavian Pavilion at the World's Fair in Osaka, Japan. Here the sound is produced by six tape loops of different playing time. It will take 102 years for all the possible combinations to be played, and for the tapes to meet again at the point from which they started. However, there is a concert version, *Lux and Tenebrae.* To continue the series of important works, *Greening,* for orchestra, was commissioned by the Los Angeles Philharmonic Society, *Zimbal* for small orchestra by the Oslo Philharmonic, *Spur,* for accordion and orchestra, commissioned by the Südwestfunk, Baden-Baden, and in 1977 *Be Not Affeard,* for soprano, baritone, five instruments and harp, was commissioned by the Royal Swedish Academy to be performed on the occasion of Nordheim's election as a member of this very distinguished body.

Finally should be mentioned two creations which, more than most of the others offer proof of the breadth of Nordheim's imagination and the scope of his creative inventiveness. It is the *Sound Sculpture,* created and planned in collaboration with the sculptor Arnold Haukeland. The sculpture, which is non-representational, stands in a cultural centre for blind people in the countryside some two hours' drive from Oslo. The idea is that the sculpture is to sing, and thereby its form and material are to be appreciated through the ear. The sound is to emanate from thirteen different points on the sculpture. The technical process starts with the daylight, which sends impulses via photocells to the "music engine", which in turn elaborates the sounds, splits

Kåre Kolberg
Photo: Norsk Komponistforening

them, and carries them to the different parts of the statue. The sounds vary according to the changing intensity of the light. The title of this construction is *Ode to the Light,* and it was inaugurated at the Skjeberg centre in 1967. The other unique work of his stems from 1975, when Nordheim, on the initiative of the Norwegian Broadcasting Corporation, composed *Connections,* or *A Media Feast.* The music was to be produced from five of the most important cities of Norway, thousands of miles apart from each other, and linked together by the radio and television, directly transmitted on one evening.

Several tokens of honour have been bestowed on Arne Nordheim, the latest and most significant being an invitation to live in the Norwegian State's abode of honour, where before him the composer Christian Sinding and the poet Arnulf Øverland once lived.

Kåre Kolberg (born 1936) has sought to establish himself as a composer alongside those who are developing styles in accordance with general European trends, and in this connection he has participated in courses in Darmstadt. Since his debut as a composer in 1961 he has produced a large number of works which demonstrate to an increasing extent his ability to free himself from the bounds of tradition and convention in his progress towards a mode of expression which is both personal and effective. In the course of his development he has experimented with electronic effects and worked with more conventional material. Some of Kolberg's most significant works are *Ludus* for organ (1963/64), *Suoni* for orchestra (1965), *Studies for Five Sculptural Groups* (1966, in conjunction with Alfred Janson), *Plym-Plym* for narrator, soloists, and chorus, and *Invocatio* for eight solo voices. Two important works from 1968 are *Hakana'anit* for organ and two percussionists, and *Jaba* 768 for jazz trio, written as a graphic score. In his later years Kolberg has to a large extent devoted his time to music for radio plays, in which he makes regular use of electronic effects. In 1974 he wrote *Tivoli,* a TV opera. From 1976 dates a *Quintet for Wind Instruments.* Professionally Kåre Kolberg is, and has been since his youth, active as an organist; he has also functioned as a music critic and since 1979 he has been the president of the *Composers' League.*

Alfred Janson (born 1937) has been connected with music all his life. His mother was a well-known concert pianist, and his father (one of Norway's leading sculptors) also used to play the flute in his leisure hours. So from the moment the boy could reach the piano he played it, and showed both pianistic talent and a receptive and creative mind which gradually led him from imitating his first idols, the accordionists, to being a very able jazz player. When he was around 20, he went back to the classics, and had his debut as a concert pianist when he was 24, with definite success.

However, he did not choose that line, but took up composition. In Norway he studied Hindemith with Finn Mortensen, then he went to Darmstadt and Stockholm, but to quote his own words: "I didn't find much pleasure in the dreary and complicated-sounding serial music." His first composition, *November,* for piano, composed in 1962, was a kind of protest against this. He worked it out on the special sound qualities of the piano, urged by a strong will to express himself. Following this came a *Cradle Song* for 48 strings and soprano, *Construction and Hymn* for symphony orchestra, *Canon* for chamber orchestra + tape, *Theme* for mixed choir, organ, percussion and piano solo, and *Noc-*

turne for mixed choir, 2 celli, 2 percussion groups and harp. In addition to this Janson has written a number of compositions for the theatre and cinema.

In each of the compositions Janson develops new sides of his techniques, but what he himself considers as basic, and on which he puts particular stress, is what he calls the silhouette form: that is, the role of proportions and movement. Up to around 1970 he generally started his work by drawing lines on millimeter-paper before he started considering details and the final choice of tone material. Later he turned to more traditional ways of working, but still he often sets up a graphic design of the formal creation. In all the compositions mentioned above he shows a very developed and refined sense of sound qualities. In *Canon* traits from jazz instrumentation are evident: the use of Hammond organ, saxophone and percussion combinations. The formal idea is also original: the music, which all in all lasts 12'34", is recorded on tape for 7 minutes. When the work is performed this tape is started 4 minutes later than the live music, thus creating a very extended kind of canon. This work was created during the 1960s, before *Theme*. Also in *Valse Triste,* a composition for sound tape and jazz orchestra from 1969, his affiliation to jazz is evident.

In recent years Janson has turned extensively to stage music, both ballet, *Mot solen* (Towards the Sun, inspired by the works of the painter Edvard Munch), composed in 1969, and the opera *Et Fjelleventyr* (Adventure on the Mountain). This work was commissioned by the Norwegian State Opera for performances on the Nordic opera stages, and first performed in Oslo in 1973, with Janson's wife, Grynet Molvig, in the principal female part. His *Violin Concerto,* called *A Prelude,* is a very recent composition, as is a *String Quartet.* Besides the stage works, he has also been busy with music for theatre, radio and television. Another opera is one of his immediate plans for the future.

The reader will have noticed that quite a number of our leading composers have earned and still do earn their living as organists. As we approach the end of this survey of twentieth-century Norwegian composers, it is appropriate to mention some of the most prominent composers who are associated especially with church music.

Arild Sandvold (born 1895) studied first at the Oslo Conservatory and later in Leipzig, under teachers such as Karl Straube, Robert Teichmüller and Paul Graener. He has been active as an organist in Oslo since 1914, and from 1933 to 1966 he held the posts of organist and precentor at Oslo Cathedral. As principal organ teacher at the Oslo Conservatory since 1917, he has tutored more or less every member of the generation of organists that has followed his own. In addition to these activities he has, for more than 30 years, also been the leader of two of the most important oratorio choirs in Oslo.

Arild Sandvold has been composing, and composing productively, from a very early age. To begin with he wrote secular music — chamber music and an orchestral suite — but from about 1920 he began concentrating more and more on church music. Over the years he has composed a large number of works for organ, as well as motets and cantatas, and unaccompanied choral works, among which we find adaptations of Norwegian folksongs. Several of his cantatas have been written for special occasions: consecrations of churches, for instance, and jubilees such as the centenary of the foundation of the Norwegian Mission Society in 1942, for which Sandvold wrote a cantata with orchestral accompaniment.

Ludvig Nielsen (born 1906) also studied at the Oslo Music Conservatory, where one of his teachers was Arild Sandvold. He also studied in Leipzig under Karl Straube, and for composition under Günther Raphael. Since 1935 Nielsen has been organist and precentor at the Nidaros Cathedral in Trondheim, where he also conducts the boys' choir, the cathedral choir and the St.Olav Choir. He has firmly established a choral tradition which involves annual performances of Bach's Christmas Oratorio and the two Passions. Considering all his activities in this respect, his productivity as a composer would naturally be restricted. Therefore he took up composition with special energy after he retired from his position at the Nidaros Cathedral.

Nielsen stresses the great influence that J. S. Bach has had on him as a composer. Even though he has in his compositions introduced into the traditional tonal system features from ecclesiastical modes, features which also appear in Norwegian folk music, in his style he has remained faithful to what Bach's church music has taught him. This is definitely the case with his large works for choirs, soloists and orchestra, such as *Te Deum,* op.9, composed in 1944/45, the *St.Olav's Day Mass,* op.11 (147/48), *Fagnadssongar* (Hymns of Delight), op.16, composed during the years 1954–57, and *Draumkvedet,* a liturgical oratorio for 2 choirs, 2 organs, barytone solo, recitation and speaking choir, where he makes use of the four folk tunes from the great epic poem. In 1963, a year or so after he had finished the oratorio, he also composed a *Passacaglia* for organ, an enlarged version of the prelude of the oratorio.

Of his most important compositions from later years ought to be mentioned a *Concerto for Organ and String Orchestra,* in the form of 9 variations and fugue on the St.Magnus Hymn from the Orkney Islands, his op.25.

As his most important work from the 1970s the composer regards his op. 42, *Lilja,* composed over a monumental poem from the 14th century. Compared to most of his other works this is written for a modest ensemble: mixed choir (not necessarily large), chamber orchestra with an extended percussion group, organ, a barytone soloist and one recitor. Of even greater importance is his tonal language in this work, regarding both structure and polyphonic elements. The tonal language is also particularly free and more contemporary in character.

Several of his works are written for and directly commissioned by his choirs or other bodies active in the musical life of Trondheim. His opus 37, *Under the Church Vaults,* was commissioned by the Municipal School of Music, and created for young people in the form of a liturgical service, using quite a large body of performers: choir, group of soloists, string orchestra, wind instruments, organ, a liturgist and community singers. He has composed several works for the Boys' Choir of the Cathedral over the years. One of the most important is *Jubilus Cordis Voce,* composed in 1977. In 1979 the choir commissioned another work, based on the introductory lines of St.John's Gospel. The work deals with the battle between light and darkness, Christ and humanity. Some of the organ parts demand highly developed virtuosity. Besides the performance in the cathedral, the choir had it on its programme on a tour through England in the same year. Nielsen's latest large-scale work to date is *Psalm 150,* for three choirs, brass, organ and harpsichord.

Per Hjort Albertsen (born 1919) is another Trondheim organist who has made a name for himself as a composer. But unlike Ludvig Nielsen he has concentrated on secular music at least as much as on church music. His teachers in composition have been the Dane Sven Erik Tarp and later Hans Jelinek in Vienna, under whose tuition he made a special study of dodecaphony. Besides his service at the Church of Our Lady he has been active in several fields of secular music life in Trondheim, first of all as a choral conductor.

Hjort Albertsen's early production as a composer is to a fairly large extent based on influences from Norwegian folk tunes, as one can hear from his *Piano Sonata* and the two choral ballads, *Bendik og Årolilja,* his op.1, and *Villemann and Magnill.* Both are based on the most famous poetry we have left from the Middle Ages, and the very choice of themes would lead naturally to the use of a musical idiom common in the nationalists' style in the 1920s and 1930s. Later divertimento elements, like those taken up by French and Danish composers, began to play a more important part in the style of his music. Examples of this trend are the *Concertino for Flute and Orchestra,* and the *Sonatina for Clarinet and Piano.* In the 1960s he worked quite a lot with music in schools, and this has brought him into contact with the theories of Carl Orff. Some of the works he has written in this field are *Småburleik,* op. 32, *Old King Cole,* and other pieces for performance in schools, including a school opera.

Of his church music *Masses,* one for Christmas and one "Summer-mass", must be mentioned.

Turning to Hjort Albertsen's instrumental works, we find a *Violin Concerto,* a *Piano Sonata,* as well as *Symphonic Prelude* from 1951 and *Overture* from 1958, both orchestral works, as is *Tordenskioldiana* from 1972. Among his works from the 1970s is *Toccata, Chaconne* and *Fugue* from 1976, one of the few works for his own instrument.

The career of *Rolf Karlsen* (born 1911) in many ways appears as a parallel to the first two composers named in this group. He had his musical training at the Music Conservatory in Oslo, the city of his birth, and his teacher was Arild Sandvold. He later devoted all his services to the capital, where he has held the position of organist in several churches before he was appointed organist and cantor of Oslo Cathedral, as the successor of Arild Sandvold. He continued directing choral societies mainly occupied with performances of oratorios and other forms of church music, and he also created new bodies, the most important of which is *Musica Sacra,* an organisation aiming at the renewal and reinvigoration of church music. As was the case with his colleagues mentioned earlier, the time available to him for composing came to be restricted, as a result of his devoting his time in so many ways to the musical life of both Oslo and elsewhere. Still there are, apart from a great variety of works directly for liturgical or ecclesiastical use, free compositions, works such as his *Easter Cantata* for 4 choirs, organ and orchestra (1965), or *De Profundis,* Introduction Chorale and Fugue (1977), composed for the celebration of Musica Sacra's 25th anniversary, or *Partita* for Recorder, Flute and Harpsichord (1979). From his earlier, "atonal" days there are a *Suite* for Piano, and one for Orchestra (1937), to mention just two.

Just as it seemed relevant to reserve a special place for some composers who, establishing their place on the musical scene during the 1930s, made their efforts in the field of church music, it seems equally right to sort out some composers who specialise in other forms of music, mainly secular, such as theatre music, dance music and jazz as a symbol of unity — exactly jazz will be a common denominator for some of them.

Gunnar Sønstevold (born 1912) was in his young days a member of the "Funny Boys", an ensemble famous in the 1930s as pioneers in Norwegian jazz. But whilst he was playing in the jazz band, he was also studying concert music — "serious music" as it was called then — and composed a number of works in a definitely serious vein: a *String Quartet,* a *Wind Quintet,* a *Sinfonietta* for orchestra, a *Concerto* for saxophone and orchestra, *Music for*

Kettledrums and Jazz Orchestra, the last one of course a sort of bridge between his two activities. There are also two *Ballets,* one connected with mediaeval Norwegian poetry, "Bendik and Årolilja", the other based on Shakespeare's "The Tempest". Further to this he has also written quite a lot of music for the theatre and the cinema.

All the time he kept pace with new developments, but in the year 1960 he went with his family to Vienna, primarily in order to study twelve-tone technique with Hans Jelinek. They stayed there for nearly 7 years, during which time his daughter developed into a first class harpist and his son into an equally skilled bassoon player, and they are now well established as prominent instrumentalists, active in leading symphony orchestras. The fourth member of the family, his wife *Maj* (see below) penetrated into her artistic field. Back home in 1967, Gunnar was for some years in charge of music for Norwegian television, and later he founded a music school together with his wife, both of them still remaining active composers. During the Vienna years he finished his Concerto for saxophone and orchestra, and since he has also composed a *Concerto for Flute and Bassoon,* a *Ballet,* "Peer Gynt", and *Rituale.* Maybe his most important work is *Litany in Atlanta,* (based on Dubois' poem), originally meant for amateur performers and modest performances, but as the work grew in formal expansion, so did the demands on the performers, in quality as well as quantity. For that reason the work had to wait for many years to be given an equivalent performance. Several piano pieces and some chamber music complete the list of Sønstevold's works.

Maj Sønstevold (born 1917) started her musical career in connection with jazz and light music, just as did her husband (to be), but, as already mentioned, they both widened their artistic scope through intensive studies. Maj Sønstevold has shown a creative power which is just as decided when it comes to simple popular songs and light music as it can be in works of larger and more complicated structure. *Nine Haikus,* Japanese poems for alto, flute and harp, op.5, from 1966, *Vårvon* (Promises of Spring), for two men's choirs, solo tenor and orchestra, and *Silence* for eight voices and an instrumental ensemble of six members are among her best-known works. When it comes to music for theatre, film, TV and radio she has been extremely productive, partly in collaboration with her husband, as in the case of the music for the TV production of *Benoni and Rosa,* from 1975.

Sverre Bergh (1915–1981) is another musician who started his career as a performing artist, and who remained one to a very great extent. He worked as a pianist, and was for nine years resident pianist and leader of the dance orchestra of the Norwegian Radio Corporation. In 1957 he became the conductor of the National Theatre's Orchestra in Bergen, until in 1976 he became director of the Bergen Festival. As a composer he studied under Arild Sandvold and Fartein Valen, and his compositions for orchestra and chamber music are written in a free style verging on atonality without being bound directly to serial technique. In this connection a *Concerto for Clarinet and Strings,* the often played orchestral suite *Småbyskisser* (Village sketches), a *String Quartet* and a *String Quintet* should be mentioned. His operetta from 1944, *Three Old Maidens,* brought him one of his first solid successes. All through his career as a composer he created works for theatre, film, TV and radio, such as his TV opera *Lyrikkens Verkefinger* (literally "Poetry's Swollen Finger") from 1974.

Finn Ludt (born 1915) has been an active musician, and music critic, but he has devoted much of his time to composing, and his production ranges from simple popular songs to music in larger forms, such as music for 9 ballets, a considerable amount of music for theatre, and two operettas: *Når kvinner ikke vil* (Lysistrata) and *Trost i taklampa* (text: Alf Prøysen). There is a *Piano Sonata* and a *Piano Suite* and many fine songs. In these works, not least the earlier ones, one notices a nationalistic tone. This is very noticeable in the romances, where the impression of nationalism is reinforced by the composer's choice of texts, taken from the poet Olav Aukrust. When composing "functional" music, Ludt has above all sought to adapt his style to the style and content of the work he happens to be writing for.

In the previous edition of *Norwegian Music,* from 1971, the present chapter closed with brief mentions of some composers who were at that time at an early stage of their careers. Today they have fulfilled the expectations we had to them. Since 1971 a series of new names has appeared on the musical scene, and it is only natural that we should look at them to see how they manage to consolidate the progress made by the pioneers we have dealt with, to what extent they have learned from their musical forebears, and whether they themselves will blaze new trails in Norwegian music. Apart from one or two of the composers to follow now, they all belong to a generation born in the 1940s and 1950s.

Also among them there are some who, through their activity as church musicians, have to a certain extent been influenced by this type of music. On the other hand there are those who have a definite secular point of departure. As jazz has come to be an increasing part of music life, and is considered more and more as just as "serious" as the kind of music earlier given the monopoly of this standard of value, it is only natural that this kind of music will be found to be essential for many of the composers to be dealt with in the rest of this chapter. Nevertheless it will be more appropriate *not* to divide them into such groups, but rather to follow a strict chronology. This will be based on the year of birth, although it might in some cases have been more relevant to take the years in which the composers made their first public appearances, since some have waited longer than others — for various reasons — before making their debuts.

One feature may strike us, and that is the number of composers who assert themselves in this period. There is no reason to believe that there has been a sudden explosion of talent. We have to look for other reasons, and two or three will probably strike us. One is that everyday use of music, that is to say serious music, is steadily growing, and this again has made the commissioning of works more and more common. Already among the composers treated earlier we have seen examples of this, when it comes to music for theatre, film, TV and radio, but the further the equipment for mechanical reproduction is developed and brought to perfection, the more it is taken into use, as specific staging of dramatic or other scenic work, as a matter of course, demands specially composed music.

A second contributory factor has no doubt been the consolidation and expansion of the activities of the organisation *Ny musikk* ("New Music" — also a branch of the ISCM). Whereas the Composers' League obviously has to look after the interests of all its members, the *Ny musikk* includes within its membership a group where active composers in what is called their "Phase of Establishment" can be accepted, provided their works pass the examination of the group's selection committee. One task of the group is to distribute commissions to their members, and the effectiveness of this is partly assured by the fact that today more funds are granted by bodies such as Norsk Kulturråd (the Norwegian Cultural Council).

A third contributory factor is the development of educational opportunities during the 1970s, through the foundation of Norges Musikkhøyskole (Norway's Music Academy) — an internationally recognized institution at university level. The Head of its Faculty of Composition, Finn Mortensen (see p. 95) is a name we will meet frequently when discussing the education of the next group of composers.

There is no doubt that the senior member of this group is *Oddvar S. Kvam* (born 1927). Despite his prolific musical talent, he was supreme court barrister before his first compostitions appeared. He studied composition with David Monrad Johansen and later in Copenhagen with Herman D. Koppel. His production has now reached opus 60, and includes orchestral works, music for various chamber music groups, and a rich body of music for all kind of choirs. Several times he has won prizes in contests for choral composition, and two of his orchestral works also won prizes in a contest held to celebrate the opening of the Oslo Concert Hall in 1977. *Opening,* his op.28, actually *was* the opening item of the inaugural concert. Kvam has written two *Symphonies,* the first of which has the subtitle "Three Contrasts" and the second "Communication". His *Concerto for Piano and Orchestra* has the title "Suffragette", and a work for choir and orchestra is named *Epinikion.* Other works which should be mentioned are *Ostinato Festoso, From the Young People's World* and *To Kill a Child,* for recitation and orchestra.

As a pupil of Monrad Johansen, it is only natural that Kvam's first compositions had a strong national colour, not least because for songs he had chosen texts from a definite nationalist among the poets, Olav Aukrust. Gradually influences from Bartók and Prokofiev can be traced. Twelve-tone music only appears rather casually, as is the case with concentration on sound effects. Kvam may be characterized as a moderately modern composer, without following any narrow stylistic trend in his modes of expression.

In the musical life of Norway Kvam has occupied several honorary positions, such as Vice President of the Composers' League, President of Ny Musikk, and in the period 1972–77 Chairman of the Board of the Philharmonic Society in Oslo.

Ketil Hvoslef (born 1939) has shared the fate of C. P. E. Bach, or – to stay within his own borders, Johan Kvandal. Just as Kvandal did not like the idea of being Monrad Johansen II, so Ketil Sæverud changed his surname to Hvoslef. The benefit of being Harald Sæverud's son was the chance of growing up in an intensive musical atmosphere, where the creating of music was around him and where, in his everyday life, he became intimate with music and musicians from near and far. However much this has influenced his start as a composer, his progress has passed through a short period when he composed very much under the influence of the Viennese school, after studying in London under Henri Lazarof. Most remarkable in this respect is his *String Quartet* No. 1, from 1969, the only work where dodecaphony is strictly carried through. However, he looks at this as a product of his final years as a student. After the early 1970s he actually returns to an idiom more like that of his first compositions. Hvoslef will not restrict himself to any defined style. He prefers to use simple and direct means of expression, because he wants to make unhampered musical contact with his fellow beings. He considers it unimportant if such means of expression are 100 years or just one day old. His point of departure will be the demands of any new creative work he wants to produce, and this decides the choice of form and the means of expression.

An important work in his later production is *Mi-Fi-Li,* composed in a special technique of variation which he also uses later. Instead of handling the musical core in an extrovert manner, he lets it influence the surrounding material and lead this inwards, towards the core. A composition for organ, *Organo Solo,* also

116

from the early 1970s, is directly related to music he wrote for a theatre performance, something which has been the case even with others of his works. It is interesting how in 1975, in *History of The Poet Lin Pe and His Tame Crane,* composed for TV, he uses the hardingfiddle (se p.11) in an untraditional way, connected with the mystery of the East and eastern ornament, rather than with Norwegian mountains and fjords. Some years later he had his most demanding task as a theatre composer, in connection with the TV production of Olav Duun's «Medmenneske».

A number of works in larger forms have appeared in the later 1970s: *Concerto for Cello and Orchestra,* and *Variations for Chamber Orchestra,* both from 1976, the main theme of the variations being gradually built up during the Concerto. His *Concerto for Orchestra* from 1979 was honoured the following year as «The Work of the Year». From 1979 dates also his *Concerto for Violin and Pop Band,* where he wants to combine his own idiom with the sounds of a pop band and what the amplifiers can add. In some of his works Ketil Hvoslef has shown special interest in instrumental song technique, first in his probably most popular work *Kvartoni,* from 1974, for soprano, recorder, guitar and piano, later in *Trio for Soprano, Contralto and Piano,* and in *Concerto for Choir and Chamber Orchestra* from 1977. Up to 1982 his latest and largest work along this trend is a choral choir opera, *Narkis and Eko.*

Trygve Madsen (born 1940) belongs to a family with rich musical traditions, and started his musical career early. He studied composition in the town of his birth, Fredrikstad, with Egil Hovland, and continued his studies at the Academy of Music and Fine Arts in Vienna from 1969 to 1971. Just like the previous composer, Trygve Madsen does not adhere too narrowly to the question of style, but rather to writing music which he can expect to be comprehensible to his audience. His tonal language is based on free tonality, and his freedom in expression may in his case be the result of many impulses, both from musical and from extra musical sources. For the latter he feels deeply obliged to the Austrian philosopher Rudolf Steiner. From Steiner he has learnt to evaluate his own lifework objectively in the light of the philosopher's thoughts. The musical sources of impressions he feels are many, covering a wide field: Austrian traditions ranging from Beethoven and Schubert to Bruckner and Mahler; the Russian school, with particular stress on Shostakovich; and Maurice Ravel. He also has a definite· affinity to jazz. In Madsen's earlier production it is not least songs which play an important role. Later he has more decidedly turned to instrumental music, in a variety of combinations: *Sonatas* for Violin, Flute, Clarinet, Oboe, Horn, Bassoon and Piano, *Concertos* for Piano, Oboe, Clarinet and Tuba, with Orchestra. Among his latest works is a *Sonata* for Tuba and Piano. His op.31 is a *Fancy* for Hardingfiddle and String Orchestra, so his interest in the different instruments and their possibilities is vivid. For theatre, radio and TV he has written music on many occasions.

Per Christian Jacobsen (born 1940) has an ecclesiastical background. He graduated as organist and cantor from the Music Conservatory of Oslo in 1965, and has since been active as a church organist. He took up composition in the 1960s, studying with Finn Mortensen in Oslo and completing his studies in this field in Copenhagen, Warsaw, Leningrad, Moscow and Zagreb. In his compositions Jacobsen has paid great attention to polyphony, and since 1976 he has been *amanuensis* at the State Music Academy with this discipline as his speciality. He received his diploma for composition in 1972, but already two years earlier he had caught attention through his motet for 12 voices, *Dömen Icke,* where he combines choral recitation, the technique of sound-blocks, and phonetic use of texts. In another choral work, *Et Facta Est Lux,* from 1972, he has combined the mediaeval Olav's hymn "Lux illuxit" with today's musical idiom in a successful organic way. Also traits from our folk music play a role, even used as direct material, as is the case in *Partita for Organ,* based on the folk tune "Se solens skjønne lys og prakt". In other works we meet melodic details with a definite Norwegian folk tune character, as in *Kontra* B.A.C.C., or the piano piece *Mellomspill* (Interlude).

Gradually new traits come into the picture: in an 8 voice motet *Et Tre* (A Tree) biotonality is involved; in another work, also from 1976, *Antitheta,* for 11 instruments, he uses self made synthetic types of scales, something which manages to add an almost extra-European character to the work. Even if as a principle Jacobsen keeps to tonalities, he is experimenting with techniques of non-tonal origin, and of definite importance generally is the stress laid on rhythmic elements.

John Persen (born 1941) qualified both as an agronomist and as a schoolteacher before he went from the northernmost part of Norway to the capital in 1969 in order to take up the study of music seriously. His teacher came to be Finn Mortensen, and he graduated from the State Academy in 1972. Later he widened his musical horizon by taking part in summer courses in Darmstadt, under the tuition of Ligeti and Kagel.

Persen reflects both in his personality and his music a mentality common to a group for whom political and racial problems are fundamental to most of their behaviour and attitudes. This is reflected in Persen's music, which shows evidence of his strong engagement in the case of the Samer (a minority population group in the extreme northern part of Norway).

He won the first prize in the competition for a composition to be performed at the opening of the new Concert Hall in Oslo in 1977. The title in Sami language was CSV, which stands for "Dare to show that you are a Same". According to the composer he does not want to write "aesthetic, beautiful music": he wants it to be "naked and brutal". He certainly used the orchestral forces to the utmost in this respect, adding a gun shot at the end. Another of his sensational orchestral works has the title *Øre-verk;* which has a double meaning. "Øre" means "Ear", but "Verk" can mean "Work" as well as "Pain". So the listeners can make their choice.

Besides orchestral works, where the stress is on sonorous structures, Persen has also composed works for choir and chamber music, as well as an opera *Under Kors og Krone* (Under Cross and Crown) from 1979, and another opera is on its way, dealing with a revolt by the Samer in Kautokeino (one of the central places in Finmark).

Now we turn to *Folke Strømholm* (born 1941). From the chronological order it is just by chance that this composer happens to stand next to the previous one, but in this case there could well be an idea behind it. The native music of the Samer has been decisive for Strømholm too. Although he started his career with a diploma from the Music Faculty of Oslo University, and afterwards studied electronic music in London and the Netherlands (his tutor was Kotonsky) he has up to now not left any work in this field, nor does he generally show any inclination towards avant-garde tendencies. On the contrary, what engaged his interest was the Joik, a speciality within the folk music of the Samer, and on the basis of free tonality he has developed a personal style, where monotony, and the extatic, are important factors. The Joik is in several cases the direct nucleus of works, as in *Samisk Overture,* his op.20, *Samiædnan* (Land of the Samer), op. 24, from 1971/72, or *Joiker* for piano, his op. 26 and 33, and a *Wind Quintet No. 2,* op.28. Among the principal works of a different character is *Water,* op. 27, with the subtitle A Phenomenological Study for Piano, composed in 1973. It is reminiscent of another piano work from 1966, *Cosmorates,* not only in terms of its musical expression, but also because of the special technique of notation employed in an attempt to bring the printed notes into accordance with the music itself. For the same instrument he has, in his *Farewell to the Piano,* op.32, from 1976, tried out new ways of exploiting the distinctive quality of the piano.

Magne Amdahl (born 1942) belongs to the group of composers who have grown from a solid root in practical, one might say service-bound activity. Apart from performing, he has written music for 35 theatre pieces, several films and more than a hundred songs. On his way over to the serious side of music he started in 1970 a series of short pieces for each instrument in the orchestra, which were performed on the radio, with the composer at the piano. For the Broadcasting Orchestra he has also written a couple of works in the light music category. Thus he was an accomplished artist in handling the sound material of the orchestra when in 1980 he wrote his *Symphony No.1, Elementum,* and the year after his *Piano Concerto No.1.* It is to be expected that we will find him belonging to the group of composers who keep to free tonality, and also that his music may be labelled as neo-romantic or even — to use another label — "new-friendly". According to Amdahl himself, Bartók and Stravinsky have had most influence on him.

Jon Mostad (born 1942) started his career as a composer around 1965, with *Poem* for piano, followed by other works for this instrument. Up to the year 1979 practically all his works are non-cyclical, but gradually he turned to composing for orchestra and other more extensive instrumental combinations. From a style based on free tonality and counterpoint he reaches a more romantic way of expression, where sonorous elements count more. This we meet in his *Song for Orchestra,* from 1973. The development goes further into a system of chords built on the row of overtones, combined with free tonal melodic lines. One of his most ambitious works was composed between 1973 and 1975, for mixed choir, 4 trombones, 2 percussionists, organ, and strings, mainly on biblical texts and pictures, planned for performance on television. Another important work is *Towards Equilibrium,* for orchestra, composed in 1980, and the cycle for organ *I'm getting ready for the Marriage Feast* . . . Here each part may be performed separately, but there are also indications of crisscross combinations designated in order to make the work a complete experience.

Jon Mostad has put particular effort into creating works meant for amateur bodies. We met this trend in the composers Egil Hovland and Finn Mortensen. The latter has no doubt also persuaded his many students at the Academy to follow up, as the demand for such music was decidedly felt, in order to make the public familiar with music from its own time, and not only aquainted with it, but ready to meet and absorb it in even more elaborated forms.

Magne Hegdal (born 1944) made his entrance on the musical scene as a pianist, but at the same time studied composition with Conrad Baden and with Finn Mortensen, ending up with a diploma from the Music Conservatory of Oslo. Besides works for piano solo he has composed *Übung,* for 2 pianos and orchestra (1977), and, two years earlier, a *Sinfonia* for orchestra. There are also compositions for choir, and for solo soprano with piano and percussion. The aleatoric principle plays an important role in Hegdal's music. In his work *Herbarium,* 45 short pieces for piano, he says: "Neither the individual parts nor the whole are intended to convey the impression of a development over a period of time.

The pieces stand here, for inspection as it were, and the whole is a result of such constantly new inspections."

Ragnar Søderlind (born 1945) has studied composition with Conrad Baden in Norway and Erik Bergman and Joonas Kokkonen in Finland. He has attempted the most diverse styles and forms, ranging from Gabrieli to Schoenberg, from Shostakovich to the Beatles, and is a follower of Mozart's words: "All that lies before me is mine." Such was his attitude as a young man, he refused to ally himself to any school of music, and tried to avoid assimilating techniques of composition which are directly linked to the personalities of other composers.

His most important compositions from his younger years are *Rokomborre* (1967), *Fantasia Borealis* (1969), and *Polaris* (1970), three orchestral works which are all inspired by the landscape of northern Norway. In the decennium to follow his production is rich, not least in its variety of forms. This is partly due to the fact that the composer received a number of commissions from institutions as well as specific performers. There are the TV opera *The Blue Serenity* and the ballet *Hedda Gabler,* based on Ibsen's drama, created for and performed by the State Opera Ballet in 1978. The music of this ballet has also been adapted for concert performance as a symphonic poem. Further, Søderlind has, during the 1970s, composed two *Symphonies,* a *String Quartet,* and a *Quintet for Brass Instruments,* a *Cantata* for choir and orchestra, commissioned by the Rikskonsertene (see next chapter), and another ballet, based on Sigrid Undset's "Kristin Lavransdatter" will appear during 1982.

Whereas Søderlind's musical idiom in his earliest compositions was atonal, he has since come to use a more moderate tonal language, as a reaction to the intellectual attitude of the 1950s. In his Symphony from 1975 he builds on the classical sonata-form, and regarding expression it may well be labelled Neo-romantic.

Olav Anton Thommessen (born 1946) is one of the most colourful among the young generation of composers, and one who, through his extensive and meticulous education and far-ranging experience, has gained a solid integrity regarding the choice of personal style, or use of means of expression. He left the Univer-

Olav Anton Thommesen   Photo: Norsk Komponistforening

sity of Indiana, USA, in 1969 as a Bachelor of Music/Composition. One of his teachers had first of all introduced him to Hindemith's music, whereas the teacher who came to mean most for him, Jannis Xenakis, opened his mind farther – to use Thommessen's own expression: "He shattered my horizons".

In those days Thommessen also became familiar with "Musique concrète" and no doubt his inclination goes towards the sonorous side of music, and all the possibilities at hand in our time to enrichen this field. This became evident from his earliest works, like *Vårløsning* (Outburst of Spring), from 1969. In his compositions *Litt Lyd* (Some Sound) for orchestra, and *A Concert — Chamber* for soprano and chamber ensemble, both from 1971, he has summed up the roles each instrument has as components of sound. A consequence of all this was his search for really profound knowledge, which brought him to the Instituut voor Sonologie in Utrecht, a centre for research into the very meaning of sound in 1972–73. Back in Norway, he launched a similar kind of workshop at the State Academy of Music, in collaboration with Lasse Thoresen (see below).

Thommessen is a very productive composer, whose works mirror a combination of rich fantasy and alert, reflective intelligence, resulting in a deliberate choice of idiom, which again directs his stylistic trend. A general trait in his music is the developing of a form through a kind of chain principle. Basic elements, "Musical mobiles", are carried on in sizable combinations. Thommessen is a firm believer in music's prime importance being communication. Not seldom is one of his works a kind of preparation for the next, and it is remarkable how inspiration from non-European music is traceable in some works. The rhythmic element prevails in some of his compositions, particularly from the period up to the middle of the 1970s. As examples can be mentioned *Opp-Ned* (Up-Down) and *Gjensidig* (Mutual), both from 1972/73. Another example is *Stabsarabesk* for military band, which through its obsessive rhythms and dynamic power is grotesque, almost barbaric in character. When played by a symphony orchestra its title is *"Barbaresk"*. This work has since been adapted for symphony orchestra. From 1974 is also *Kvadratspill* (Quadratic play) for 4 percussionists, where obviously the rhythmic aspect will be the more pronounced. This will also be the case in still another work from that year, *Maldodor/Hunhaien* (The Female Shark) for percussionists and two actors. This is part of *A Chamber Opera about Desire*, of which 3 of 4 parts are now ready.

As a reaction to the previous rhythmically rather eruptive works, he goes over to make use of more lyrical and only subtly dynamic means of expression. In one of the latest works his idiom has grown impressively rich in dimension as well as variety. The title is *Macrofantasy for Piano and Large Symphony Orchestra on Grieg's A Minor*. However great the difference is otherwise, the fullness of the orchestral sound as well as the use of the solo instrument may evoke in one's mind a Liszt or Mahler.

Tommessen has of course written music for stage and film,

also special works in connection with pedagogic purposes, such as *Nok en til* (Still another one) for wind quintet, with commentaries, or *A Poster-Opera for Music* (both from 1978/79), the latter composed for the State Opera School. His ever flourishing, versatile fantasy brought forth another fruit on the vocal side in 1980: *Et Glassperlespill (A Game of Marbles)* for choir and orchestra, in which both music and text are signed O. A. Thommessen.

Gunnar Germeten jr. (born 1947) felt — like some of his contemporaries — the necessity of acquiring a thorough knowledge of the complete sound material at hand for a composer today. Consequently he found his way to the Instituut voor Sonologie in Utrecht, after having graduated from the State Academy of Norway in 1947, where his principal teacher was Finn Mortensen. With a Dutch state scholarship he studied W. Kaegi and G. M. Koenig in Utrecht under 1975 and 1976.

One of the earliest works of importance among Germeten's creations, *Tilfellet Janice* (The Case of Janice) from 1974, shows his inclination for a full sonorous body, using a large symphony orchestra plus a vocal soprano soloist and a soprano saxophone. Another work along these lines is *Siokrate*, for 2 children's choirs, a ballet dancer, 2 percussionists and tape, commissioned by the Rikskonsertene in 1977/78 and performed on extensive tours arranged by this institution, both throughout Norway and in Stockholm. Most of Germeten's works have been commissioned by different organizations, such as is the case of *Akt 2*, for 6 performers, composed 1977 for the chamber ensemble of *Ny Musikk* and performed both in Norway and in several other European countries. *Sketchma* for piano, from 1980, is a commission by the Norwegian Broadcasting Corporation. *Dance through the World of Shadows* for string orchestra, a commission by the Nomus organization, had its world premiere in Helsinki. *Grex vocalis*, commissioned by the choir of the same name in 1981, was even performed in Greece. Germeten has also written music for film and a series of TV productions.

Terje Rypdal (born 1947) is solidly rooted in jazz, of the most exquisite quality. He is one of the leading jazz guitarists, also internationally, and he has composed a good number of works in that style. However, this is just one side of the composer. He has a degree in music from the University of Oslo, and has studied composition with Finn Mortensen. His debut as a composer of "ordinary" music took place in 1971, with *Eternal Circulation*. In 1972 came his opera *Orpheus Turns around and Looks at Euridice*, a work composed for the Sonja Henie-Onstad Art Centre near Oslo, where it also had its world premiere. From 1972/73 there are a *Concerto Par Violbasse E Orchestra*, as well as concertos for piano, violin, horn, oboe, accordion (title: *ABC*), and harmonica (title: *Modulation*), all of them with orchestra.

There are also several *Symphonies*. *No. 1* stems from 1975 and was composed as a commission by Norwegian television written so as to accompany a film, *Symphony No. 2* has the subtitle *New Era*, is from 1979, and shows together with the two works from 1980 *Tumulter No.2*, for percussion solo and large orchestra, and the *Oboe Concerto*, subtitled *Shadows*, Image for oboe solo, 4 trombones,percussion and strings, the full ripeness of Terje Rypdal's style. Sonority in all possible richness and variety seems to be the basic element, and apparently a composer like Penderecki has not been without some influence here. Rypdal's solid knowledge of the whole instrumentarium at hand, his sense of form as well as his prolific imagination, result in warm, colourful music. Efficient craftsmanship combined with an ability to create an organic unity of elements from the jazz and pop music with the full spectre of today's musical means of expression penetrates his music, which for him first of all seems to aim at ordinary human communication through exquisitely differentiated moods. Should any of the current labels be put on Terje Rypdal's music, it should probably be neo-romantic, and he should be regarded as a representative of "New-friendliness".

Lasse Thoresen (born 1949) has already been mentioned above, as a collaborator of Olav Anton Thommessen at the sonological workshop of the State Music Academy. Since 1975 he has been teaching electrophony and sonology at the academy, and at the same time he has been undertaking research work for the Norwegian Research Council for Science and the Humanities. From 1973 he has been engaged, together with Thommessen, in the development of a music theory based on analyses of sounding music, rather than the written picture of it. For his own creative work, as a composer, he is aiming at the choice of sound materials which avantgardism has brought about, as a result of its experiments. He wants to make this part of miscellaneous structures, whose models are taken from traditional music. Also elements of folk and art music from other countries are sometimes incorporated in his works. His continuous occupation with electrophony has been important also when it comes to instrumental compositions, or to combining both in one work. This is just the case with his "multimedia" work *Skapelser* (Creations) from 1978, for a chamber ensemble consisting of violin, clarinet, soprano, marimba and vibraphone, together with tape and film, a ballet commissioned in connection with the celebration of the 10th anniversary of the Sonja Henie-Onstad Art Centre. It has since been produced as a TV ballet.

Apart from *Skapelser,* the following work is among the most important on his rather extensive opus list: *Hagen* (The Garden) for soprano, violin, cello, piano, and 2 percussionists. This work was commissioned by the Composers' League and had its world premiere at the inauguration of the chamber music hall of the Oslo Concert Hall. Thoresen composed this work during 1975/76, basing it on a text by Abdu'l-Bahá. Quite a number of his compositions have a sacral or spiritual character, and he often finds his inspiration or chooses his texts from the Bahá-i writings, such as in the case of *Velatus,* for mixed choir, commissioned by Det Norske Solistkor in 1976. From 1980 dates a series of works: *Stages in the Inner Dialogue,* for piano, *Origins* for bassoon concertante, double bass and vibraphone, and *Dråpa* (an old Norse poem) for flute and harpsichord. *A Trio for Piano, Violin and Cello* will soon be added to the list.

Synne Skouen (born 1950) grew up in an atmosphere of diverse musical activities. From 1969–73 she studied composition at the Academy of Music in Vienna under, among others, Alfred Uhl and Dieter Kaufmann. The latter taught experimental composition and acquainted her with the French school of "musique concrète". Tradition as well as the avantgarde made their impact. In Vienna she also met with the ideas of Hanns Eisler, which, according to her, became influential. Back in Oslo she continued her studies with Finn Mortensen at the Norwegian State Academy of Music, where she obtained her diploma in 1976.

Today's musical "pluralism" may seem to offer itself to the composer like some kind of a supermarket. Synne Skouen maintains that this calls for an acute awareness of the purpose of music and significance of genre, form and technique. In her music the diversity of musical "style" can be heard either by way of different techniques placed right next to and "commenting on" each other, or contrasting within the same part. She is aiming at neither diversity as such, nor at synthesis, but at ambiguity of expression.

Among the works of Synne Skouen are: *Tombeau to Minona* (1976) for large orchestra. The year after she produced a "mini-cabaret" entitled *What did Schopenhauer say. .? An argument in score.* Essential in her production so far is music in connection with other media, such as film, TV and radio (the TV-ballet *Evergreen* from 1979; the audiovisual composition *Pregnancy – A Voyage through unknown Country,* a groupwork from 1980/81; and the solo pianopiece *Hail Domitila!* commissioned by the radio in 1980). She frequently uses electro-acoustics in combination with instrumental music. Since 1981 she has been concentrating on different works in collaboration with the author Cecilie Løveid. She first created the music for a radio play of hers. Next came a trio, *Rye* for soprano, cello and piano, based on Løveid's lyrics. Furthermore the two of them are collaborating with the artist Marianne Heske on a piece of musical theatre involving video, two players (a soprano and an oboist), electro-acoustical soundscreen and instrumental ensemble, to be produced in 1983.

Guttorm Kittelsen (born 1951) has from his very young days been active in performing music, be it in school band, pop or jazz band. However his development turned more and more to the serious and professional side. After music line of college he studied at the Oslo Conservatory and later at the State Academy, where he received his MA diploma as flutist in 1976, and two years later in composition, as pupil of Finn Mortensen.

Even if flute came to be his principal instrument, he also devoted himself to Guitar, Double bass, and not least the electronic instrumentarium, strongly convinced of the importance these instruments will obtain in the music of future years. Consequently he feels it his duty to create music for them which can put them on a real artistic level, make them accepted within the field of "serious" music. Elements of this we trace in his *Kyrie* for choir and orchestra from 1974, and explicitly so in *Oppfinnelse Nr. 5* (Invention No. 5) for percussion and electronics (1981) or *Movements, 2nd version* from the same year.

Halvor Haug (born 1952) has been trained as a composer in Norway, at the Sibelius academy in Helsinki, and i London. Out of great respect for tradition he started in a rather conservative way. First of all his concern was to make his music sound "professional", to use his own word. He used polyphony to a large extent, and translucent orchestral sound and clean melodic line prevail in his earlier compositions. As for his basis of harmony, he has — like several of his contemporaries — chosen "free tonality". Gradually the polyphonic side has grown less pronounced. His most important works include *Symfonisk Bilde* (A symphonic Picture) from 1976, composed at the request of his fellow composer and conductor Ragnar Søderlind. It is an attempt to give a picture of what symphonic music is, by melting into an entity the different compositorial techniques. The year after came his *Symfoniske Konturer* (Symphonic Outlines), and in 1980 *Poema Pathetica,* which is an orchestral version of his chamber work *Symphony for Five,* of 1979. Also from 1980 is another symphonic poem, *Poema Sonora,* commissioned by the Oslo Philharmonic Society, to be performed by its orchestra in the autumn of 1982. There are a number of chamber music works in addition to *Symphony for Five* (for flute, clarinet, horn, guitar and piano), including a *Brass Quintett* from 1981. One of his earliest works was a *Sonatine* for violin and piano (1973).

Magnar Åm (born 1952) is a new example of a composer with solid anchorage in church music. Trained and active as an organist, he studied composition in Bergen with Ketil Hvoslef, and later in Stockholm with Ingvar Lindholm. His view of musical creation goes hand in hand with his philosophy of life, and if we compare with what his teacher Ketil Hvoslef stands for, we will see to what extent they resemble each other: Åm has declared that for him it is essential to find an inner relationship, leading to understanding: the relationship between the sound values at every level, and the forces this can produce both in himself and in the listener have meant more for him than searching for new sounds, new ways of using the instruments, or new ways of appealing to the audience. The majority of Åm's works are somehow connected with the church, and often they are first performed by bodies of performers connected with it. Exceptions are some of his orchestral works: *Bønn* (Prayer) for mixed choir, soprano solo and string orchestra, from 1973, *Study on a Hymn Tune from Luster* (a district in the western part of Norway) for string orchestra, from 1979, and *Zero,* for choir, children's choir, soloists, orchestra and organ, from the same year, a work where the density of melodic lines has reached a climax in his work to date. In *På Glytt ...* (Ajar. . .) for double bass and orchestra, commissioned by the Bergen Symphony Orchestra and performed there in 1981, he has added a folk tune, to be sung. Noticeable in this work is also the fact that the clarity is greater in every respect. His latest work is *Burfugl's Draum* (Dream of a Bird in Cage), written for a moving choir, violin, soprano solo, two percussionists, double bass, electric guitar and piano. To this he has added the projection of slides. In this work we may find definite traits of Bulgarian folk music, and also some from jazz.

Kjell Samkopf (born 1952) is a composer whose musical background should predestine him for the rhythmical side of music. He started as a drummer in his local boys' brass band, and is today a tutor for percussionists at the Conservatory of Eastern Norway. In the course of his career he has studied and taken his diploma at the State Academy, studied at the Instituut voor Sonologie in Utrecht (1978/79) and even had an extended period of study in the USA, at the Creative Music Studio, New York. He divides his time between being a performing musician and a composer. Like many others of his contemporaries he has been a pupil of Finn Mortensen at the Academy, which he left with a diploma in composition in 1977. His earliest work which should be mentioned is an *Overture* for Symphony Orchestra from 1976, but when we examine his list of works further, we find that percussion instruments and the use of electrophony occupy a central position. There is a *Concerto for Vibraphone and Strings* from 1977, *Oppfinnelse* (Invention) No. 3 for piccolo flute and percussion from 1979, *Oppfinnelse* No. 4 for two percussionists and electrophony from 1980, as well as an *Oppfinnelse* No. 5 for percussion and electrophony from 1981. Samkopf says about Oppfinnelse No. 5 that it is an attempt to reach a uniform musical language where elements from different types of music create a totality. Oppfinnelse No. 4 likewise contains elements from several sources, from serial music as well as rock, sound structures typical of serial music are interwoven with rhythmical patterns from rock and jazz. In the two parts there is a free and a rhythmical part. Within each formal element the performers are free to improvise over a given material. The work is concluded with a Coda, consisting of electrophonic sounds, realized by means of computers. Thus, this is not only contemporary music, but has exciting perspectives for the future.

Kjell Habbestad (born 1955) studied church music at the State Academy in the years 1975 to 79, and composition with Finn Mortensen from 1979 to 1981, when he received his diploma. His works up to now are mainly of ecclesiastical character, but are penetrated with a will to renew it through manysided use of the rich choice of compositiorial "raw" material of our time. In works like *Om de siste ting* (About ultimate matters) or *Påskekantate* (Easter Cantata), thought for everyday use and relatively traditional in character, he combines late Norwegian romanticism with jazz improvisations, aiming at the creation of a new style in church music. In other works he builds on free improvisations for the performers, even choir and scenographic elements. Two works, *Jubal I* and *Jubal II*, are a kind of "Gesamtkunstwerk", where different forms of communication are present: recitation, song, dance and scenic presentation in simple, stylized movements. Ideas from the antiphony of the Renaissance and early baroque have given inspiration. The performers are supposed to be spread over the entire church, from gallery to altar and pulpit. The music is first of all to give colour to the happening, and material of different styles, including folk music from different countries, is used, the technique of quotations playing a definite role. The works mentioned are all from the year 1981, and point clearly to his future trend.

Yngve Slettholm (born 1955) has, like Kjell Samkopf, firm roots in wind music, though this time in connection with the Salvation Army, where he started playing the horn when he was 6 years old, and his activity as a performing musician — and conductor — has been within the same framework. He started studying composition in 1978 at the State Academy, with Finn Mortensen as his tutor, and he received his diploma in 1980. He eventually changed his main instrument from the horn to the flute, which he studied with Finn Henry Olsen at the Academy, and later with Ørnulf Gulbransen.

Even if he wrote some compositions before 1978, he feels himself that his real years of ripening and development started when he came under the guidance of, and got the solid support of, Finn Mortensen. During the years 1978/80 he developed from a neo-classical and tonal way of composing into a style more influenced by serialism. We can mention three stages, represented by *Four Profiles,* for solo saxophone (1978), *Magma,* for piano (1979) and from the same year 13 *Monomanias,* short aphoristic pieces for wind sextet in a style which seems to express great admiration for Webern.

The first works after his departure from the Academy are written for the kind of performers he was closest to: for example *Sigma* from 1980, for band – this time seemingly marked by the influence of Messiaen, who had caught his vivid interest at that time. From 1981 there are two works for wind ensembles: *Di-vision* for a brass ensemble of 10 players, and *Hymn,* for school bands. Since that time he has again turned to the saxophone, his latest work to date being *Introduction and Toccata* for saxophone and percussion, the latter consisting mainly of 4 timpanis, which do not serve just as accompaniment, as the work has more the character of a duo for the two performers. His next work is to be for symphony orchestra.

———————

And now this chapter will be concluded with a definite Benjamin in this brotherhood of composers.

Nils Henrik Asheim (born 1960) was educated as a church musician at the State Academy. Simultaneously he studied composition for several years with Olav Anton Thommessen, who — consistent with expectation — had rather strong influence on him. He consciously used his first independent period as a composer to liberate himself from this sufficiently to find his own personality, though at the same time he cherished all the valuable help given him. He had already started composing at the age of 13, and has ever since been active. A lot of his music is written for chamber music combinations, and maybe his first work we should dwell on is in this field: *Ensemble Music for Five,* from 1977, a work which has gained solid recognition and has been performed quite frequently, also internationally, since it won the second prize at the "Rostrum of Composers" in Paris in 1978.

As was to be expected, the works gradually to come are composed for ecclesiastical use. *Midt iblant oss* (Amidst us) from 1978 is the result of collaboration with an artist, the work being intended for performance in a church where slide reproductions of the artist's water colour paintings are to be synchronized with the music. *Orgelleik* (Organ play) is a virtuoso number for that instrument, whereas *Gud miskunn* (God have mercy), his most ambitious work up to now, represents a one hour meditation service with music especially composed for it. The work is comparable to a classical Mass, but here the text is especially written for this work. The music is in a dialogue relationship to the text, and its function changes correspondingly.

CHAPTER SIX

MUSIC IN NORWAY TODAY

During the first half of our century steadily growing developments had come to the fore on the musical scene in Norway. These developments came to an abrupt stop with the German occupation in 1940, which completely lamed public musical activities for 5 years. The majority of the population boycotted all such activities in protest. On the other hand, the activity behind the blackout curtains increased considerably. Music in homes and private circles reached proportions which had been unknown for almost a hundred years. It was evident that making music and listening to it offered relaxation and a break in the tension that were badly needed those days.

But this type of musical activity was not able to continue once the country was free. After the Liberation musical institutions and organisations that had existed before 1940 became active again, and new ones joined them. During the early postwar years the enthusiasm for music which had begun during the occupation provided a firm basis for further development. There is a striking difference between the situation in 1945 and that of 1918: during the First World War Norway had been neutral, and had enjoyed a high degree of prosperity that entailed the giving of large private donations to music: but in 1945 the means for reorganising and developing musical activity had to come from public sources, either from the State, or the local authorities, or other economically viable institutions.

This is, to quite a large extent, the situation today. When one considers what has been achieved since 1945, one has to bear in mind Norway's geographical difficulties, her sparse population and her comparatively short existence as a free nation. We have to accept the fact that development here is slower than in countries with a denser population, better economic conditions and much longer traditions. Nevertheless, developments since the

War are definitely promising, not least because they have as their starting-point a vigorous interest in music among the general public. Apart from professional music, which centres on the larger cities with their symphony orchestras and regular recitals given by concert performers, there are local musical societies, amateur orchestras, choirs, bands and so on. So we can quite justifiably speak of nation-wide musical *life*. There are a number of national organisations in which these amateur bodies are re-presented, and these in turn are affiliated to a central institution called the Organisation for Popular Musical Activity (Det folkelige musikkliv).

Such, then, is the breadth of Norwegian musical life. Its high points are naturally to be found in large cities, with their symphony orchestras, and especially in the capital, where we also find Norwegian State Opera, and the State Academy of Music, which was established in 1972.

The symphony orchestra in Oslo is run by the Philharmonic Society, which has existed as such since 1919. But the Society's history in reality goes back to the previous century. Many attempts were made to keep an orchestra going in the capital, always mostly with amateurs. In 1871 Edvard Grieg and Johan Svendsen consolidated it, and the Musikforeningen which they created is the direct predecessor of the Philharmonic Society. When this was formed in 1919, its orchestra consisted of 59 musicians. The present orchestra (as of 1982) is composed of 83, but as from the autumn season of this year the orchestra will be enlarged to 90 musicians. Before 1977 the orchestra had to have its concerts in the Aula of the University, with a seating capacity of around 800 and with a rather narrow platform, something which hampered the development of the size of the orchestra. Since Oslo acquired its new Concert Hall in 1977, seating around 1 500, the orchestra has had sufficient space for further development, and is hopefully looking forward to reaching in the not too distant future the number of performers normal for a full symphony orchestra today.

The concert season in Oslo lasts from early September until the beginning of June. The orchestra gives about 60 public concerts (subscription series, special concerts, performances for

Oslo Philharmonic Orchestra   Photo: Arne Svendsen

young people and so on) and in addition it has to play up to 250
hours for productions by the Norwegian Broadcasting Corporation. The bulk of the programmes for the public concerts is from
the standard, rather conservative repertoire. In the new concert
hall the orchestra has been able to extend it by performing larger
works like the 8th symphony of Mahler and Verdi's Requiem,
because the space permits it. In addition to its Oslo activities the
orchestra goes on tour both within the country and abroad. Up
to 1968 the orchestra had as permanent conductors and artistic
directors three Norwegians: Olav Kielland, Odd Grüner-Hegge
and Øivin Fjeldstad. Later several conductors of foreign origin
have had this post, which is currently held by the Russian Mariss
Jansons.

The symphony orchestra of Bergen, whose official name is
Musikselskabet Harmoniens Orkester, is not only Norway's but also
one of the world's oldest existing music societies, founded in
Bergen in 1765. Before the orchestra was reorganized in 1919, it
was — just like the *Oslo Symphony Orchestra* — subject to periodic
fluctuations. From 40 members in 1919, the orchestra today

Musikselskabet Harmoniens Orkester   Photo: Norsk Telegrambyrå

numbers 69 permanently employed musicians. The orchestra has very varied range of activity: in addition to subscription concerts there are special concerts for groups of the society, from children to elderly people, district concerts, and also some touring, and at the end of each season the orchestra is one of the backbones of the Bergen Festival (q.v.). The Bergen Orchestra has, during the last 10 years also been able to change from a rather unsatisfactory cinema for its concerts to the magnificent and acoustically very successful Grieg Hall, with a seating capacity of around 1600. For the last 18 years the permanent conductor and artistic director of Musikselskabet Harmonien has been the Norwegian *Karsten Andersen.* It is not unreasonable to think that this may have had a certain influence on the choice of programme, which has reflected a particular interest in contemporary Norwegian Music.

The history of the *Trondheim Symphony Orchestra* goes back to 1909, but it is only since the end of the Second World War that it has been established as the city's permanent symphony orchestra. The Norwegian Broadcasting Corporation played an important part in this development by starting a chamber orchestra in Trondheim consisting initially of 15 strings. Later the orchestra was expanded by the addition of wind players, and gradually it has taken on the shape of a symphony orchestra. In 1982 the number of musicians, full-time professionals, has grown to some 58–60. Every season the orchestra gives around 70 concerts of various types, and in addition around 80 studio productions for the Broadcasting Corporation. This orchestra also plays for the Norwegian Opera when it comes to Trondheim on tour one or two times per season. The orchestra's permanent conductor and artistic director for more than 30 years was *Finn Audun Oftedal,* who was succeeded in 1982 by the Czech conductor *Jiri Starek.*

The fourth of Norway's symphony orchestras which is organised on a permanent residential basis is the *Symphony Orchestra of Stavanger,* and here the situation is in many ways similar to that of Trondheim. The core of professionals in the orchestra was for a long time the Stavanger Ensemble, employed by the Norwegian Broadcasting Corporation. Gradually it was completed by part-time musicians in order to give symphony concerts in the city. Today the orchestra is made up of 56 musicians, 38 of them employed full-time. At the same time this orchestra functions as the Stavanger Radio Orchestra. The permanent conductor and artistic director for a good number of years has been *Bjørn Woll.*

Evidently all the four symphony orchestras mentioned regularly perform the large works which, besides the orchestra, also need bodies of choral singers. The two societies first mentioned have their own choirs: the Oslo Philharmonic Choir was founded in 1921, and the Choir of the Bergen Music Society *(Harmoniens kor)* was founded as a separate unit within the Bergen Music Society in 1857. Today both choirs number some 100–110 members. We have already heard that all the orchestras mentioned produce programmes for the Norwegian Broadcasting Corporation in some form. This is not only necessary for their existence: we may as well say that it is necessary or at least of great importance for the keeping up of the musical culture on this level nationally. Due to the difficult geographical conditions of the country, this is the only way the Norwegian population gets an overall chance to listen to symphonic music.

Since the economic situation has made it necessary to maintain this cooperation between the Broadcasting Corporation and the orchestral societies, the Norwegian Broadcasting Corporation itself does not have a real symphony orchestra. The *Kringkastingsorkestret* (Broadcasting Orchestra) was founded in 1946 in order to serve as a light music and dance orchestra. Gradually it has grown from 36 to 50 musicians, full-time professionals, and its function as a dance orchestra ceased a long time ago. Besides concerts, with a wide repertoire, the orchestra produces music in connection with all sorts of other programmes: ballet, theatre pieces, documentaries, shows etc. Its permanent conductor through more than 30 years was *Øivind Bergh*, now it is *Sverre Bruland*.

The orchestras mentioned (and that of the State Opera) are the only ones in Norway that are organised on a permanent basis, with support from the State, the local authorities, and the Broadcasting Corporation. But there are numerous towns throughout the country with their own symphony orchestras, composed mainly of amateurs. These musicians, who generally perform under professionally trained conductors, work with a purposefulness and idealistic fervor which lead to very commendable results. The number of performances can vary from one season to the next, these orchestras often collaborate with choirs in presenting large-scale oratorio performances. Of great importance for these activities is a national organisation which is given support by public authorities so that it can hold annual courses where young members of the various local orchestral societies come together in order to receive instruction from professional musicians. During these courses the young musicians join together to form the Norwegian Youth Orchestra, *Ungdomssymfonikerne,* which gives concerts under the direction of the permanent artistic leader of this undertaking, *Karsten Andersen*. The results achieved are today of such a high quality that this orchestra can present works like Stravinsky's "Rite of Spring" at a definitely professional standard, and being performed by the only really fully developed symphony orchestra (some 120 members) of Norway, these concerts have become real events. These courses are organised by the Norwegian Musicians' Union, and the youngsters who get the chance to participate are to quite an extent students training for professional status; thus it actually serves as an orchestral training camp. Now there are also similar camps arranged by the Norwegian Association of Amateur Symphony Orchestras, where the training is more or less the same, but evidently the skill of the participants on their respective instruments is not quite so highly developed.

Norway's geographical conditions make it inevitable that there should be numerous towns and cities that are not large enough to have orchestras like those we have mentioned, but where the need for direct contact with music is just as great as, say, in Oslo or Bergen. For these places, tours by professionals, either individuals or small groups, have been of great importance. For a long time these tours were arranged by the musicians themselves, and through the years many performers have taken a lot of trouble to provide music in circumstances which were by no means ideal, considering the difficult communications and the lamentable premises and instruments they had to contend with. But things have now taken a turn for the better, and conditions have been improved by more efficient organisation. Tours are now arranged by local concert societies which are affiliated to a nation-wide organisation called *The Friends of Music*. For some years now this association has been doing splendid work in arranging tours and collecting founds to provide decent instruments for the travelling musicians.

Further to this, since 1968 musical activity throughout this vast, sparsely populated country has received vital support from *Rikskonsertene* (The State Foundation for Nationwide Promotion of Music). The field of activity of the Foundation includes the following: evening concerts, school concerts, tours to health and social institutions, the arranging of other organizations' productions both inside Norway and abroad, an artist exchange programme with other countries, and the arrangement of trial concerts for chosen debutants. The Foundation also functions as a guarantee against financial loss at debut concerts, it offers instruction on a nationwide and regional basis, and provides general services for the entire country's musical activity.

Today, the institution is the country's largest employer of performing musicians engaged on a short-term basis. In 1979

Kirsten Flagstad   Photo: Norsk Telegrambyrå

there were about 9 200 concerts given by over 800 artists. These concerts reached a public of approximately 1,143,700. The *Riks-konsertene* also have a hand in performances by local orchestras, choirs and chamber ensembles, as well as performances given in collaboration with the Norwegian State Opera, *Den Norske Opera.*

We have mentioned this institution several times, but what position does it occupy on the contemporary musical scene? In the first place it is the opera of Oslo, its permanent residence, where the highest number of potential consumers are. Nevertheless part of its activity takes the form of tours to other parts of the country, as well as performances outside Norway. As a public institution, receiving support from the State and local authorities, the opera is young: it gave its first performance in February 1959, with Kirsten Flagstad as its first director. The Opera's

From Tchaikovsky's "Eugen Onegin" at Den norsk Opera   Photo: Karsten Bundgaard

financial standing is, and has always been, unsatisfactory, and it has also had to contend all the time with the problems created by the lack of a theatre of its own, a fact which limits its running repertoire. But despite these adverse conditions, the Opera has managed steadily to increase its activity and expand its staff. Today there are approximately 25 vocal soloists, 45 choir members, 75 musicians in the orchestra, while the solo dancers and ballet corps amount to 45. Besides the director of opera, and that of ballet, there are two permanent conductors, a number of repetitors, a ballet master, and choir master, and all the personnel necessary for the running of an opera theatre.

Den Norske Opera attempts to set up a versatile programme with emphasis on the international standard repertoire, but also contemporary music drama has been given a position of gradually growing importance. This also applies to Norwegian works, some of which are commissioned by the Opera. In 1980 the number of performances on the Oslo stage amounted to 137, and in addition came other arrangements in the capital (49 of them), as well as 59 performances outside Oslo.

The Norwegian National Opera also runs a ballet school, whereas the education of operatic singers is entrusted to the State Opera School, and since the ballet school of the Opera is only for children and does not directly aim at professionalism, there is also now a State Ballet School, which offers vocational training at an advanced level. The State Opera School today has a broad curriculum, and its goal is to offer education in the following areas: solo and ensemble singing, musical drama for radio and televison, operetta and musicals, and music for future regional theatres. This school was founded in 1964, while the State Ballet School is only 2—3 years old.

When the Norwegian State Opera was established in 1959, it was not a completely new venture, for the Norwegian Operatic Society had been giving performances both in Oslo and in other places around the country for a number if years since 1945, when Gunnar Brunvoll launched this undertaking and kept it going mainly on the basis of private support, but with a little help from the official authorities. Before 1940 a number of operas had been performed at the Oslo and Bergen National Theatres,

From Arne Nordheim's "Stormen" at Den Norske Opera   Photo: Karsten Bundgaard

and these theatres continued to present operas even after the foundation of the Norwegian Opera. But Norway and her capital had not had a permanent opera company since the years immediately following the First World War, when the "Opéra Comique" was established in Oslo during that period of great national prosperity. Although the Opéra Comique survived for only a few years, it gave a good number of memorable performances, with soloists including Kirsten Flagstad, who had previously made her debut as a 16 year old girl at the National Theatre in Oslo in d'Albert's "Tiefland".

It remains to mention one more organisation which plays an active and regular part in providing music: *Ny Musikk* (New Music Society), which is the Norwegian branch of the ISCM (International Society for Contemporary Music). Ny Musikk is a

The Grieg Hall, centre of the Bergen Music Festival   Photo: Norsk Telegrambyrå

nationwide organization, run by artists, of which the primary aim
is the dissemination of knowledge about Norwegian and foreign
contemporary music. As a society, with regular meetings and
arrangements for its members, it works for the development of
forms of presentation and musical expression which have not

been dealt with — or only to a very small degree — by other institutions. It arranges concerts and in similar ways supports creative and performing musicians, as well as attempting to improve their economic and professional situation. As the Norwegian section of the ISCM, it takes care of the Norwegian interests connected with the ISCM and international music cooperation generally.

A recent extension of the society's activities is the foundation of a special Composers' Group, comprising active young composers, who are still establishing themselves. An important part of their activity is the distribution of commissions, arranging special concerts and other forms of propaganda work. Through discussions, lectures etc. they establish a fruitful milieu for development.

At this point we leave the organizations which provide music on a more or less regular basis. But during the last fifteen to twenty years major musical events, concentrated in short spaces of time, have been taking place in Norway. The most important and most comprehensive of these is the annual *Bergen Music Festival,* which takes place in the second half of May and the first few days of June. Since its inauguration in 1953 the Festival has developed into one of the big events in Norwegian musical life, as well as becoming a truly international festival of music, not only because of the numerous participants from abroad, but because it is internationally known and attracts audiences from all over the world. In recognition of the value which the Bergen Festival has as a manifestation of our cultural life, the Government grant awarded to it has increased over the years to such an extent that it is now possible to go to such ambitious lengths as commissioning operas, ballets and symphonic works. It is also possible to have several guest orchestras at the Festival every year, and those invited are among the best in the old and new worlds. Top international artists — soloist as well as chamber ensembles — also appear regularly, but it is only natural that Norwegian music and musicians should play a major role at the Festival, and one of the aspects of the occasion which the visitors from far and wide appreciate most, is the chance to meet Norwegian artists at the informal concerts that are held every day during the Festival at

Edvard Grieg's home Troldhaugen, some five or six miles outside Bergen.

The Troldhaugen recitals are only one of the events. The arrangements totally include symphony concerts, chamber music, intimate, church, and jazz concerts, opera and ballet performances, folk singing events, folklore, art exhibitions, films, and seminars. In 1980 the active participants numbered 1 500, with about 110 different arrangements.

Festspillene i Nord-Norge (The North of Norway Festival) is arranged in much the same way as the Bergen Festival, but on a more modest scale, and with a greater degree of participation from local sources. The festival is primarily aimed at presenting art and culture in Harstad, as one of the central towns of North Norway, and provides a forum for artists from this part of Norway. To quite an extent its goal is to stimulate amateur activity. In 1980 there were about 80 arrangements.

In the field of jazz, festivals are held regularly in the towns of Kongsberg and Molde. In the course of the last ten years the jazz millieu in Norway has flourished, and the jazz festivals attract a steadily growing public. The *Molde International Jazz Festival*, first arranged in 1961, was among the first jazz festivals to be organized in Europe. The Festival's programme spans most of the styles within jazz. A large number of internationally known jazz musicians have visited Molde, and the wide spectrum of Norwegian jazz has been presented as well. In addition, other art forms are gradually being included in the Festival, such as theatre, ballads, folk music, classical music and visual art. The *Kongsberg Jazz Festival* is the other of the two big Norwegian jazz festivals. Ninety per cent of the music played at this festival is contemporary music and for the most part the participating groups, both Norwegian and foreign, are completely new. This festival was arranged for the first time in 1965.

This publication has first of all dealt with music created in Norway. This last chapter – and also part of the first chapter — have been dedicated to the re-creation of music. The quality achieved in this respect is of course dependent on the possibilities of education. There is no reason to believe that Norewegians are any less talented as musical practitioners – either as creative or as interpretative artists — than people of most other nationalities. Given this, there are two factors which must be considered: the standard musical knowledge an average Norwegian will obtain through the normal school curriculum, and on the other hand how highly developed and comprehensive the education is which a potential musician can obtain in his choice of music as a career in his own country.

The answer to the first question will be that the situation will differ quite a lot depending on where in the country a person goes to school, as well as how many years he spends there. There is a basic school system which is compulsory for 9 years. In its curriculum a certain amount of music making — singing first of all — has its place. Then from a certain point the pupils are allowed to choose between music and other so called "free" subjects. If a pupil shows particular interest and ability he may choose a special course of study in the secondary school where music is central in the curriculum. For those who do not want to go through the 3 years of secondary education, there is a system of district music schools, conservatories, where they are able to cultivate their special interests. Amongst other aspects of activity, these conservatories offer vocational training to educate orchestral musicians, singers, instrumental or song teachers, and they also provide preliminary courses before further study at the Academy of Music.

A State Academy of Music has only existed for some 10 years, but during that time it has developed to a standard completely fulfilling the demands made on such an institution, and fully comparable to equivalent institutions in other countries, both when it comes to the breadth and height of the education given. The Norwegian State Academy of Music is affiliated to the Nordic Council for Music Conservatories, Académies de Musique, and Musikhochschulen of Europe, as well as the International Society for Music Education (ISME), of UNESCO.

Karlsen, Rolf 111
Kielland, Olav 66, 136
Kittelsen, Guttorm 128
Kjellsby, Erling 81
Kjempevise 14
Kjerulf, Halfdan 24 ff
Kolberg, Kåre 105–106
Kongsberg Jazz Festival 147
Kringkastingsorkestret 139
Kvam, Oddvar S. 115–116

Langeleik 10
Lasson, Per 48
Lie, Harald 79
Lie, Sigurd 48
Lindeman, Ludv. M. 10, 21 ff
Ludt, Finn 113
Lur 9

Madsen, Trygve 117–118
Molde International Jazz
    Festival 147
Mortensen, Finn 95–96, 98, 106,
    118, 119, 121, 125, 126, 128,
    130, 131, 132
Mostad, Jon 121
Munnharpe 10
Musikselskabet
    Harmonien 136–137
Myllarguten 20

Neverlur 10
Nielsen, Ludvig 108–110
Nordraak, Rikard 26f, 29
Nordheim, Arne 100–105
Ny Musikk 144–146
Nystedt, Knut 86–88

Oftedal, Finn Audun 138
Olsen, Carl Gustav Sparre 62–64
Olsen, Finn Henry 132
Olsen, Ole 43
Oslo Philharmonic
    Society 135–136

Persen, John 119

Rikskonsertene 140
Rypdal, Terje 125–126

Samkopf, Kjell 130
Sandvik, O. M. 30
Sandvold, Arild 108, 113
Schjelderup, Gerhard 48
Seljefløyte 10
Selmer, Johan 35f
Sinding, Christian 40 ff
Skouen, Synne 127
Slettholm, Yngve 132
Slåtter 11, 19, 46
Sommerfeldt, Øistein 66–67
Springar 15
Stavanger Symphony
    Orchestra 138
Strømholm, Folke 119
Svendsen, Johan 32 ff, 135
Sæverud, Harald 73–76, 116
Søderlind, Ragnar 122
Sønstevold, Gunnar 111–112
Sønstevold, Maj 112

Thommessen, Olav
    Anton 122–125, 126, 133
Thoresen, Lasse 126
Thrane, Waldemar 17
Troldhaugen 146–147
Trondheim Symphony
    Orchestra 137–138
Tveitt, Geirr 64–65

Ulfrstad, Marius Moaritz 65 ff
Ungdomssymfonikerne 139

Valen, Fartein 53–57, 79, 113

Winter-Hjelm, Otto 32
Woll, Bjørn 138

Åm, Magnar 129

Addendum to
Kristian Lange: NORWEGIAN MUSIC
INDEX

Albertsen, Per Hjort   110
Alnæs, Eivind   48
Amdahl, Magne   120
Andersen, Karl   80–81, 91, 100
Andersen, Karsten   137, 139
Arnestad, Finn   84
Asheim, Nils Henrik   133

Backer Lunde, Johan   49
Baden, Conrad   82, 100, 121, 122
Berge, Sigurd   98–99
Bergen Music Festival   146–147
Bergen Symphony
   Orchestra   136–137
Bergh, Sverre   113
Bergh, Øivind   139
Bibalo, Antonio   93–95
Borgstrøm, Hjalmar   48
Brevik, Tor   83–84
Bruland, Sverre   139
Brustad, Bjarne   69–71, 82, 83,
   91, 97, 100
Bræin, Edvard Fliflet   82–83
Bull, Edvard Hagerup   92–93
Bukkehorn   10
Bull, Ole   19ff, 27

Cleve, Halfdan   48

Den Norske Opera   141–144
Draumkvede   14

Edda   9, 14
Egge, Klaus   76–78, 95
Eggen, Arne   49–50, 57, 79

Festspillene i Nord-Norge   147
Fjeldstad, Øivin   136
Flagstad, Kirsten   141
Fongaard, Bjørn   91–92

Gangar   15
Germeten, Gunnar   125
Gjallarhorn   9
Grieg, Edvard   7, 13, 15, 26,
   29 ff, 135
Groven, Eivind   15, 60 ff
Grüner-Hegge, Odd   136
Grøndahl, Agathe Backer   38
Gulbransen, Ørnulf   132

Habbestad, Kjell   131–132
Hall, Pauline   88–90
Halling   15
Halvorsen, Johan   42, 45 ff
Hardingfele   9, 61, 65
Haug, Halvor   129
Hegdal, Magne   121
Holter, Iver   44
Hovland, Egil   96–98, 117, 121
Hurum, Alf   51
Hvoslef, Ketil   116–117, 129
Haarklou, Johannes   43–44

Jacobsen, Per Christian   118–119
Janson, Alfred   106–107
Jensen, Ludvig Irgens   67–69
Johansen, David Monrad   40,
   58–60, 79, 115
Johnsen, Hallvard   85–86
Jordan, Sverre   79–80